LIBRARIES NI
WITHDRAWN FROM STOCK

NORTHERN IRELAND

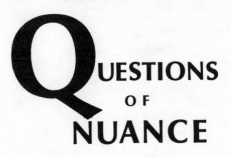

QUESTIONS OF NUANCE

PADRAIG O'MALLEY

D1354680

THE
BLACKSTAFF
PRESS

BELFAST

First published in 1990 by
the John W. McCormack Institute of Public Affairs
of the University of Massachusetts at Boston

This edition published in 1990 by
The Blackstaff Press Limited
3 Galway Park, Dundonald, Belfast BT16 0AN, Northern Ireland

© Padraig O'Malley, 1990
All rights reserved

Printed by the Guernsey Press Company Limited

Typeset by Textflow Services Limited

British Library Cataloguing in Publication Data
O'Malley, Padraig
Northern Ireland : questions of nuance.
1. Northern Ireland. Politics
I. Title
320.9416
ISBN 0-85640-454-3

CONTENTS

PREFACE

This report looks at the development of political attitudes among the political parties in Northern Ireland, the Republic of Ireland, and Britain since the New Ireland Forum to the end of the eighties. It does not take account of the tentative prospects of talks that began to emerge in the opening weeks of 1990. However, even if "talks about talks" do get off the ground and lead to more substantive negotiations, the underlying rationales the constitutional parties will fall back on, the assumptions that will inform their negotiating strategies, and their perceptions of their own actions and motives and the actions and motives of their protagonists will be firmly anchored in the evolution of their own attitudes during the eighties, especially in the years since the signing of the Anglo-Irish Agreement.

These interviews will, I hope, provide an overview of the situation and a range of voices – some harsh, some conciliatory, some truculent, and some gentle, some open to change and some closed to it – that will help each player to understand the actions of other players. Most parties proceed from starting points that are far apart, and thus, one of the report's conclusions: "… [T]here is, at least, some common ground: All parties to the conflict believe negotiations should be going on. But who should attend these negotiations, the areas of discussion they should involve, how talks should be structured, how the process itself should unfold, and under whose auspices talks should be held are questions over which there are widespread differences. Moreover, both Unionists and Nationalists have widely different perceptions of the events of the last four years and the respective reasons why they and their opponents should come to the table. Furthermore, there is a fundamental and perhaps insoluble difference regarding the purpose of talks themselves ..."

It is my fervent hope that talks do get under way and that many of the observations in this report regarding the obstacles in the way of such talks either become redundant shortly or of minor significance.

The interviews which form the core of the report were carried out in November and December 1989, with two exceptions. My thanks to all who participated for their courtesy and thoughtfulness, for making the time available when it was often inconvenient for them to do so, and for giving considered responses to my questions rather than rehashing old shibboleths. My sincere thanks to the late Harold McCusker who, though severely ill, insisted on going ahead with the interview. He died a few days before this report went to press.

Also, my thanks to Ed Beard, Director of the John W. McCormack Institute of Public Affairs, and the staff of the Institute, in particular, Mary-Beth McGee, for support and encouragement. Thanks, too, to Patricia Keefer for her in-depth comments on an early draft. And finally, Marcy Murninghan's editorial skills and painstaking transcription of the interview tapes have added immeasurably to the lucidity of the report.

PADRAIG O'MALLEY

FEBRUARY 1990

NOTE

In the seven years that have elapsed since the publication of *The Uncivil Wars* much and not much have changed in both parts of Ireland. Some of the players have left the political arena, a few of their own volition and others not, while some seem to have become permanent fixtures.

Mrs. Thatcher is well into her third term as Prime Minister of the United Kingdom. In the South, Mr. Haughey heads his second government since 1987; the first was a minority Fianna Fail government, the second, a coalition of Fianna Fail and the Progressive Democrats – a party founded in 1985 by a number of Fianna Fail dissidents led by Des O'Malley.

The economy of the South has improved drastically in some regards – inflation and interest rates are among the lowest in Europe, the balance of trade has a healthy surplus, government spending and the international debt situation has stabilized. But in other regards it is worse – unemployment hovers between seventeen and twenty percent and emigration is draining the country of its best and brightest. Since 1982, upwards of 200,000 people have emigrated, forty-six thousand alone in the twelve month period that ended in April 1989.

John Hume, James Molyneaux, and Ian Paisley continue to lead their respective political parties. Garret FitzGerald, Oliver Napier, and Thomas MacGiolla, however, stepped down as leaders of theirs. FitzGerald stepped aside for Alan Dukes following the defeat of his Coalition government in the general election in February 1987; Napier resigned in 1984 to make way for John Cushnahan; three years later, Cushnahan resigned and was replaced by John Alderdice; and MacGiolla relinquished his position in 1988 in favor of Proinsias de Rossa. James Prior took his leave of Northern Ireland in September 1984. His place was taken by Douglas Hurd; when Hurd was promoted to Secretary of State for Home Affairs in 1985, the Northern Ireland portfolio was given to Tom King. King, in turn, was replaced by Peter Brooke in the cabinet reshuffle of July 1989.

Sinn Fein abandoned the Eire Nua policy of federalism in 1982, and one year later Gerry Adams became President, consolidating the Northerners' grip on power and paving the way for an end to abstentionism as it applied to the Dublin Parliament in 1986; the latter move led Ruairi O'Bradaigh and Daithi O'Conaill to resign from Sinn Fein and found Republican Sinn Fein, one more splinter group in the Republican movement. Sinn Fein struggles to keep its Armalite-in-the-one-hand and ballot-box-in-the-other-hand strategy in place but with a diminishing degree of success. In the North, electoral support has leveled off at roughly one-third of the Nationalist vote; in the South, it is virtually non-existent.

John McMichael of the Ulster Defence Association was assassinated in December 1987; months later, Andy Tyrie – under pressure and increasingly the point man for accusations of racketeering in the upper echelons of the leadership – stepped down as the organization's Supreme Commander. Robert McCartney was expelled from the Official Unionist Party and went on to found the Campaign for Equal Citizenship, a quasi-political organization which held that the people of Northern Ireland were being denied equal citizenship in the United Kingdom because they could not vote for the mainland political parties – the parties of British government.

In the South, the voters went to the polls four times, twice to amend their constitution and twice to elect a new government. In September 1983, they approved by a two-to-one margin an amendment to the constitution to prohibit abortion; in June 1986 they rejected by a roughly similar margin an amendment that would have removed the constitutional prohibition against divorce legislation, despite the pleas of FitzGerald ("We have seen the tragedy in our past on our island of a majority saying 'No minority rights'. Are we in the Republic different? Have we the foresight to say 'Yes' to minority rights?") that Protestants in Northern Ireland would be closely watching how the South voted.

In the North, the Northern Ireland Assembly, which had been stillborn with the refusal of the SDLP to take their seats, and had never gotten beyond the point of being a Unionist talking shop, was abolished in 1986 at the end of its first term, and the Northern Ireland economy began to improve in 1988 and 1989 after the unemployment rate finally peaked at twenty percent in October 1987.

A British-Irish parliamentary body, which both governments had expressed "a willingness to cooperate in setting up" during the Anglo-Irish summit in November 1981, met for the first time in February 1990. The body consists of fifty members: among the twenty-five seats on the British side are two for Unionists members of Parliament, which the Unionists have not filled, and one for an SDLP member of Parliament, which the SDLP has filled. In March 1990, the Irish Supreme Court ruled that Articles 2 and 3 of the Irish Constitution represent both a legal and political claim to jurisdiction over Northern Ireland, and that the "reintegration of the national territory" is nothing less than "a constitutional imperative". Mr. Haughey subsequently ruled out the establishment of an all-party Oireachtas committee to consider the possibility of removing or amending the articles because they gave offense to Unionists.

Undoubtedly, the most significant political event of the latter part of the 1980s, however, was the signing of the Anglo-Irish

Agreement in November 1985. The Agreement gives the South a consultative role in the affairs of the North, an acknowledgement by Britain that Northern Ireland is not the exclusive preserve of the British government. For better or worse, the Agreement has put Anglo-Irish relations in a new context.

Meanwhile, the killing goes on.

INTERVIEWEES

Unless otherwise stated, quotations are from the following interviews with the author:

Gerry Adams, M.P. *Party President*	Sinn Fein	15 Nov 89
John Alderdice *Party Leader*	Alliance Party	18 Nov 89
Peter Brooke, M.P. *Secretary of State* *for Northern Ireland*	British Government	9 Jan 90
Proinsias de Rossa, T.D. *Party President*	Workers' Party	15 Dec 89
Alan Dukes, T.D. *Party President*	Fine Gael	13 Nov 89
Garret FitzGerald, T.D. *Former Taoiseach*	Fine Gael	8 Nov 89
John Hume, M.P., M.E.P. *Party Leader*	Social Democratic and Labour Party	20 Oct 89
Brian Lenihan, T.D. *Tanaiste; Minister* *for Defence; Former* *Minister for Foreign* *Affairs and Co-Chair* *of the Intergovernmental* *Conference*	Fianna Fail	25 Nov 89
Ken Maginnis, M.P.	Official Unionist Party	8 Nov 89

Seamus Mallon, M.P. *Deputy Party Leader*	SDLP	12 Nov 89
James Molyneaux, M.P. *Party Leader*	Official Unionist Party	11 Nov 89
Danny Morrison *National Publicity Director*	Sinn Fein	8 Nov 89
Robert McCartney, Q.C. *President*	Campaign for Equal Citizenship	12 Nov 89
Harold McCusker, M.P. *Former Deputy Party Leader*	Official Unionist Party	19 Nov 89
Eddie McGrady, M.P. *Party Whip*	Social Democratic and Labour Party	12 Nov 89
Kevin McNamara, M.P. *Party Spokesman on Northern Ireland*	Labour Party (British)	14 Nov 89
Des O'Malley, T.D. *Party President; Minister for Industry and Commerce*	Progressive Democrats	8 Dec 89
The Rev. Ian Paisley, M.P., M.E.P. *Party Leader; Moderator of Free Presbyterian Church*	Democratic Unionist Party	8 Dec 89

Lord Prior *Former Secretary of* *State for Northern* *Ireland*	Conservative Party	15 Nov 89
Peter Robinson, M.P. *Deputy Party Leader*	Democratic Unionist Party	19 Nov 89
The Rev. Martin Smyth, M.P. *Imperial Grand Master* *of the Orange Order*	Official Unionist Party	14 Nov 89
Dick Spring, M.P. *Party President;* *Former Tanaiste*	Labour Party (Ireland)	13 Nov 89
John Taylor, M.P.	Official Unionist Party	14 Dec 89
Sammy Wilson *Press Officer*	Democratic Unionist Party	18 Nov 89

NORTHERN IRELAND: QUESTIONS OF NUANCE

The support for Sinn Fein in the 1982 Assembly elections made a mockery of Dublin's claim that the IRA had no substantial political base in Northern Ireland. To meet the challenge Sinn Fein's performance posed, the four major constitutional nationalist parties on the island – Fianna Fail, Fine Gael, and the Labour Party from the South, and the SDLP from the North – came together in the New Ireland Forum in May 1983 to hammer out their vision of a New Ireland. Among them these parties represented the ninety percent of the Nationalist electorate on the island who disassociated themselves from the IRA's campaign of violence. The Forum had two goals: a *political* objective to contain Sinn Fein and a *policy* objective to set forth the common agenda of Nationalists for achieving a New Ireland that would provide a clear and unambiguous alternative to armed struggle.

After eleven months of deliberations, twenty-eight private sessions, thirteen public sessions and fifty-six meetings of the four party leaders, the New Ireland Forum issued a report of its findings in May 1984.[1]

After briefly setting out the origins of the problem, the report harshly criticized British policy since 1969 for being one of "crisis management." The heart of the problem, it argued, was Britain's failure to provide the Nationalist population of the North with any constructive means of expressing its nationalism and its aspirations, thereby undermining constitutional politics.

Having set out what it called a "Framework for a New Ireland: Present Realities and Future Requirements", the Forum addressed itself to the question of options: "The particular structure of political unity which the Forum [would wish] to see established was a unitary state, achieved by agreement and consent, embracing the whole island of Ireland and providing irrevocable guarantees for the protection and preservation of both the Unionist and Nationalist identities." A new, nondenominational constitution would be drawn up "at an all-around constitutional conference convened by the British and Irish Governments."

In addition to the unitary state model, the Forum examined two other constitutional proposals: one for a federal/confederal state and one for joint authority. Under joint authority, "the London and Dublin governments would have equal responsibility for all aspects of the government of Northern Ireland", thus according "equal validity to the two traditions in Northern Ireland." Finally, the Forum said that it remained "open to discuss other views which [might] contribute to political development."

In his press conference immediately following the Forum report's official release, Charles Haughey set the record straight. The Forum, he said, called for a unitary state; only a unitary state would "ensure a durable and lasting peace and stability."[2] In short, Mr. Haughey was merely reiterating his February 1983 contention: "There is no point in having a bipartisan approach [toward Northern Ireland] if it is the wrong one."[3]

The irony was inescapable. Throughout its deliberations, the Forum had sought to appease Mr. Haughey, to modify his insistence that a unitary state was the best and only acceptable form of unity. The parties to the Forum could not publicly be seen to fail; this would almost certainly ensure further decline in the SDLP's political fortunes. And so, he wrung his concessions: the less than evenhanded analysis of the problem's origins; the harsh assessment and indictment of British policy since 1969; no reference to an internal settlement within Northern Ireland; a veto of Garret FitzGerald's wish to insert an explicit reference to Articles 2 and 3 and to express a willingness to modify them to assuage Unionist objections; and the watered-down critique of the South's Constitution. The impasse lasted until mid-April, when the only option – the unitary state – became the preferred option, although the other two were also presented as proposals to the Forum.[4]

Dr. FitzGerald was quick to refute Mr. Haughey's interpretation. The report was not a "blueprint" but an "agenda for possible action."[5] Not only were all three options on the table, but his government was ready to consider options beyond those outlined in the report.

The rift between Fianna Fail and the Fine Gael-Labour coalition became open when the FitzGerald government indicated, on 11 May, that it would seek to establish a dialogue with the British government on the basis of the "realities" and "requirements" set out in the Forum report. These were, in the words of the government's spokesman, "the building blocks ... for negotiation because they did not exclude anything."[6] The Fianna Fail response was sharp and critical; the government, it said, was "walking away from the Forum report."[7] And when Dr. FitzGerald himself openly indicated that he would favor a movement in the direction of joint authority, the rift widened.

Meanwhile, however, the real dialogue was taking place out of public view. In November 1983, Irish Prime Minister Garret FitzGerald and British Prime Minister Margaret Thatcher held their second summit meeting at Chequers, the British Prime Minister's country estate. FitzGerald made the argument to Thatcher that alienation in the minority Catholic community in Northern Ireland had reached such a high level that unless measures were taken to alleviate it, there would be serious consequences for constitutional politics in Northern Ireland. Specifically, he referred to the support that Sinn Fein had elicited in the British general election in June 1983 when Sinn Fein received forty-three percent of the Nationalist vote in Northern Ireland. He argued that if that vote got any higher, it could signal the end of constitutional politics in Northern Ireland, that if this were to happen the consequences would spill over into the South and possibly destabilize constitutional politics there, and that that, in turn, would have serious consequences for Britain.

FitzGerald came away from the meeting believing that Mrs. Thatcher had not been receptive to his argument, but he was mistaken. She concurred, in fact, with his analysis of the situation, and in March 1984, Sir Robert Armstrong, Secretary to the British cabinet, arrived in Dublin to initiate informal talks with the Irish government. Formal talks began one year later, in March 1985.

Despite the lack of success of attempted political initiatives throughout the seventies and early eighties, the political formula for an agreement was already in place. Successive Irish governments accepted that the status of Northern Ireland would not change without the consent of a majority of the people there, while successive British governments acknowledged that an Irish Dimension existed, and that a devolved government would have to have the support of the Nationalist community.

In two crucial respects, however, the capacities of both governments – but especially the British government – to translate good intentions into political actions were severely circumscribed by the entrenched, unmovable positions of their respective clients. The Unionists, secure in their constitutional position under the Northern Ireland Constitution Act (1973) and tenacious in their belief that their numbers alone precluded them from being coerced into any form of devolved government that did not countenance majority rule, or any North-South relationship that involved more than mere "neighborliness," were in a position to veto every proposal. Moreover, since their position on an Irish Dimension was absolute, the coupling of devolution that would require their making concessions on the sharing of power with the SDLP and an Irish Dimension that would involve their making concessions to the South made any progress on devolution impossible. On the Nationalist side, the refusal of the SDLP to enter into any discussion of devolution without a prior undertaking that an Irish Dimension was an issue of at least equal standing gave it, too, a veto power that led to paralysis. Accordingly, the British government's power to move the political parties in the North in the direction of an accommodation was severely curtailed. It was a zero-sum game: Anything that appeared to be acceptable to Unionists was a sufficient reason for its rejection by Nationalists, and conversely, anything that appeared to be acceptable to Nationalists was a sufficient reason for its rejection by Unionists.

The Anglo-Irish process, initiated in May 1980 by Irish Prime Minister Charles Haughey and British Prime Minister Margaret Thatcher, had resulted in a series of summit meetings in December 1980, November 1981, and November 1983 between the Prime Ministers of both countries. In November 1981, both governments agreed to establish an Anglo-Irish Intergovernmental

Council to give institutional expression "to the unique character of the relationship between the two countries."[8] The Council met on a regular basis – indeed, in one eighteen-month period, November 1983 to March 1985, it met on no less than thirty occasions. In short, the basis was laid for an institutional framework within which the Irish and British governments could accommodate their mutual interests and debate their often not inconsiderable differences on a whole range of matters, including Northern Ireland. Such institutional relationships, it was clear, were not subject to the veto powers of the Northern parties. The Anglo-Irish process, therefore, was the first step in shifting the framework for a political initiative out of the narrow confines of Northern Ireland and making it the shared responsibility of the two sovereign governments.

The summit held at Hillsborough Castle, County Down, on 15 November 1985, at which British Prime Minister Margaret Thatcher and her then Irish counterpart, Garret FitzGerald, affixed their signatures to the Anglo-Irish Agreement, was, according to the communique which followed it, "the third meeting of the Anglo-Irish Intergovernmental Council to be held at the level of Heads of State."[9]

The Agreement, which was ratified by Dail Eireann on 21 November by eighty-eight votes to seventy-five, by the House of Commons on 27 November by 473 to forty-seven, and registered under Article 102 of the Charter of the United Nations on 20 December, effectively gave Dublin a consultative role in how Northern Ireland is governed.

It is succinct, its brevity almost concealing the craftsmanship that went into its wording.[10] First, both governments affirmed that any change in the status of Northern Ireland would come about only with the consent of a majority of the people of Northern Ireland. Both governments recognized that at present the Unionist majority wished for no change in its status. And both governments promised to introduce and support in their respective parliaments legislation to secure a united Ireland if in the future a majority of the people in Northern Ireland were clearly to wish for and formally to consent to the establishment of a united Ireland. (Heretofore, communiques issued after summit meetings contained statements to the effect that both governments agreed that the constitutional position of Northern Ireland as part of the United Kingdom would not be changed without the consent of a majority of its people. A communique, however, is just a political statement and has no legal standing. An agreement between two governments, on the other hand, ratified by their respective parliaments and lodged with the United Nations, has international legal standing. Articles 2 and 3 of the Irish Constitution claim jurisdiction over the territory of Northern Ireland. A clause in the Agreement that would have the Irish government recognize the constitutional position of Northern Ireland as part of the United Kingdom would have been contrary to these two Articles, in violation of the law, and thus void. It took some time for the Irish negotiators to convince their British counterparts that neither the word "constitutional" or the phrase "as part of the United Kingdom" could be included in Article One. Also, to ensure compliance with their respective constitutional practices, two differently worded agreements were drawn up. The "Irish" version put before Dail Eireann was an "Agreement between the Government of Ireland and the Government of the United Kingdom"; the "British" version put before the Westminster Parliament was an "Agreement between the Government of the United Kingdom of Great Britain and Northern Ireland and the Government of the Republic of Ireland." Accordingly, when one talks of the status of Northern Ireland in the context of Article One, the word "status" can mean exactly what one wishes it to mean. To the Irish it means one thing; to the British another.)

Second, the two governments agreed to set up an Inter-governmental Conference that would be jointly chaired by the British Secretary of State for Northern Ireland, currently Peter Brooke, and a "Permanent Irish Ministerial Representative", at present the Minister for Foreign Affairs, Gerry Collins. The functions of the Conference would pertain both to Northern Ireland and the Republic of Ireland, specifically with regard to political matters, security arrangements, the administration of justice, and the promotion of cross-border cooperation. A provision specifying that "determined efforts shall be made through the Conference to resolve any differences" – a binding legal obligation with precedent in international law – seemed to suggest that the Irish government's role was more than merely consultative.

Third, both London and Dublin support the idea of a devolved government, dealing with a range of matters within Northern Ireland, that would command "widespread acceptance throughout the community." Should this occur, Dublin would, nevertheless, retain a say in certain areas affecting the interests of the Nationalist minority (such as security arrangements and human rights). If devolution did not come to pass, then Dublin would continue to have a say in all matters that affect Nationalists. Finally, after three years, the workings of the Conference would be reviewed "to see if any changes in the scope and nature of its activities are desirable."

Thus the logic of the Agreement and the ordering of the priorities: First, work out the relationship between the two governments on a government-to-government basis; develop a set of institutional arrangements not susceptible to the shifting vagaries of political actions in the North; and then look for an internal settlement within Northern Ireland. And thus, since widespread Unionist opposition to the Agreement was anticipated, the inducement the Agreement provides to encourage Unionists to negotiate an acceptable form of devolution with Nationalists. On the one hand, there is the carrot: The more willing Unionists are to share power with Nationalists, the smaller the role of the Conference, and hence the smaller the role of the South in the affairs of the North. And on the other hand, there is the stick: The longer Unionists refuse to share power, the larger and more long-lasting the role of the South in the affairs of the North. In this sense, the Agreement was designed to undermine Unionist intransigence.

The Agreement initially made for some strange bedfellows. Fianna Fail, Sinn Fein, and the Unionist parties opposed it with varying degrees of vehemence; the SDLP, the Alliance party, and the coalition parties in the South (Fine Gael and Labour) supported it with various degrees of enthusiasm. The British political parties, in a rare display of unanimity – and being more than willing to have Britain's Ireland problem become, in some small and more obvious measure, Ireland's Ireland problem – gave it their unconditional imprimatur.

Of particular note, however, was Mr. Haughey's opposition. "The Agreement," he said during the Dail debate on the treaty, "seeks to bolster up the political structure in Northern Ireland when that structure is the root cause of the problem ... It represents an abandonment of Irish unity and a copper-fastening of the partition of our country. It will not bring peace or stability but only serve to prolong violence and strife ... The Agreement is in total conflict with the Constitution and in particular Articles 2 and 3 ... For the first time even the legitimacy of the Unionist position which is contrary to unification has been recognized by an Irish government in an international agreement ... The British guarantee to the Unionists has been reinforced by the Irish government ... It is a triumph for British diplomacy which undermines the very basis of constitutional nationalism ... We will certainly not be prepared to accept it in its present form."[11]

In Northern Ireland, Nationalists overwhelmingly supported the Agreement and Unionists overwhelmingly rejected it. With the passage of time, however, Nationalist support has eroded – since the Agreement has made little difference in the day-to-day lives of Catholics and has failed to deliver on some of the more conspicuous promises of reform, especially in the area of the administration of justice, that were made at the time of its signing – while Unionist opposition has remained firm. One poll, taken in 1988 shortly after the imbroglio over the Stalker/Sampson report[1] and the rejection of the appeal of the Birmingham Six,[2] found that only sixteen percent of Catholics believed that the Agreement had benefited the minority community, while an overwhelming eighty-one percent of Catholic respondents could find no benefit to their community from it. Protestants, of course, found even less in the Agreement with which they could identify: Eighty-five percent of Protestant respondents believed that Protestants had not benefited from the Agreement and only a minuscule four percent could point to some benefit to their community.[12]

Nevertheless, despite opinion polls, SDLP leaders insist that the Agreement has had a more subtle psychological impact in the Catholic community. "The feeling of isolation from the rest of the country has decreased," says SDLP deputy party leader Seamus Mallon. "The impact of the Agreement has been subliminal in some way but it is very noticeable in other ways – this feeling that their [Catholics'] position has now got to be recognized and dealt with." Indeed, says Mallon, "I would always say that was my reason for supporting the Agreement – the fact that it gave a permanent presence in the North of Ireland to the Irish government through the Secretariat." Party whip Eddie McGrady characterizes the Agreement's impact in Catholic Northern Ireland a little differently – but different in a similar way. "First, there was a growing awareness that the writ of the Irish government was in fact running, to a large degree, over the thirty-two counties of Ireland. Second, that there was a mechanism whereby the problems and concerns [of Nationalists] could be addressed other than through the British administration. And third, [there was] a great hope for the future that it would grow into something more substantive and that the opposition of Unionists would dissipate."

Ultimately, of course, the Hillsborough Agreement will be judged on the extent to which it achieves its avowed aims – that is, the extent to which it promotes peace and stability in Northern Ireland and helps to reconcile the Protestant and Catholic communities, with their divergent but legitimate interests and traditions. The notion that these aims can be achieved, however, was the product of explicit and implicit assumptions on the part of both Dublin and London – assumptions that are, perhaps, not entirely tenable.

The explicit assumption was that if the alienation in the Catholic community in Northern Ireland – the result most immediately of the British government's security policies and its administration of the judicial system – went beyond a certain point, the adverse consequences for constitutional politics on the island as a whole would be not only serious but potentially irreversible. The implicit assumption was that even if there was initial widespread opposition in the Protestant community to whatever agreement the two governments came to, it would subside when the benefits of such an agreement, in the form of a lower level of violence and the formal international guarantee of the Unionists' constitutional position, became apparent to a majority of Protestants. In sum, according to the logic that prevailed, the *existing* level of alienation in the Catholic community was such as to require new political arrangements in the short run to alleviate it, whereas the *possible* level of alienation in the Protestant community was thought to be containable in the long run.

Unfortunately, even if the new political arrangements successfully addressed Catholic concerns and support for Sinn Fein began to diminish, this would provide neither a guarantee of peace and stability, nor a reduced level of alienation between Catholics and Protestants. Reforms attributed to the Agreement by the SDLP may have weaned Nationalist votes away from Sinn Fein, but this has not resulted in a decrease in the activities of the IRA. There is no *necessary* relationship between the capacity or will of the IRA to commit acts of violence and the level of political support for Sinn Fein.

On the contrary, the IRA has been able to step up its campaign of violence; in each year since the Agreement went in to effect, the level of IRA violence has exceeded its pre-Agreement levels. The number of killings in 1986, 1987, 1988, and 1989 were above 1985 levels. The IRA still strikes randomly, ruthlessly, and with little regard for life. Each new killing of a member of the Ulster Defence Regiment (UDR) (an army regiment recruited only in Northern Ireland, it is almost exclusively Protestant) or the Royal Ulster Constabulary (RUC) (the Northern Ireland Police, also predominantly Protestant) has only strengthened the conviction of Protestants – who already see themselves as the victims of a calculatedly cold-blooded campaign of genocide conducted by the IRA – that the Agreement has facilitated and encouraged the IRA. Loyalist paramilitaries are again engaging in the random assassination of

Catholics and the divisions between the two communities remain as great as ever.

As a result, the Intergovernmental Conference has often found itself pulling in two different directions at once, as it has tried to balance the British government's propensity to move slowly in the area of reform in order to placate the Protestants with the Irish government's propensity to move quickly in order to shore up whatever support the SDLP has won in the Catholic community. These dual countervailing imperatives – the simultaneous need to pull back and to push forward – have led to a number of stalemates, especially in judicial matters where the British government has not been willing to replace the one-judge Diplock Courts with a three-judge system advocated by the Irish government.

So, in terms of facts and figures and the more obvious measurements of progress – and always bearing in mind that what is progress to one community is more often than not an anathema to the other – the Agreement has hardly lived up to its early billing. Indeed, in terms of the extent to which it has achieved its principle aims, it must be considered a failure. In sum, the Agreement has not been a cure-all for Nationalist grievances and its tangible benefits are few.[3] However, to judge it in these terms alone would be to misunderstand its real purpose and the profound impact it has had on the Unionist psyche.

There can be no doubting the Agreement's historic significance. For the first time since 1920 when the partition of Ireland occurred, the British government explicitly recognized that the Republic of Ireland has a role to play in the governance of Northern Ireland – a far cry from the 1982 declaration by the Foreign Office that Britain considered itself "under no obligation to consult the Dublin government about matters affecting Northern Ireland."[13] Giving Dublin a role in Northern Ireland constitutes an implicit acknowledgement by Britain that the partition of Ireland, in political and social terms, has been a failure. For its part, the Irish government was prepared to accept explicitly the fact that Northern Ireland will remain within the United Kingdom as long as that is the wish of a majority of the people there. This amounts to an implicit acknowledgment that unification is an aspiration, not an inevitability. The Agreement, therefore, is a quid pro quo of sorts. In exchange for the Irish government's recognition that Unionists have the right to say "No" to a united Ireland, the British government was prepared to give the Irish government a role in Northern Ireland in areas relating to the aspirations, interests, and identity of the Nationalist minority.

Accordingly, the status quo that had existed from 1920 to 1985 was destroyed with two strokes of the pen, and if the Union as Unionists knew it was over, so, too, were the fanciful notions, so earnestly and witlessly promulgated in the South for sixty-five years, that only Britain's presence in Northern Ireland stood in the way of Irish unity. In this sense, the old order is dead, the Agreement being, in one sense, the plug that was pulled on the artificial, political life-support systems that were sustaining Northern Ireland, and in another sense, a shock to the body politic itself.

It is, therefore, not important whether the Agreement has a list of accomplishments to its credit that can be ticked off to show it has made good on its promises. Even in the absence of line-item successes, there is no going back to pre-Agreement assumptions or political arrangements. The Agreement will survive arguments – even disagreements over extradition, Diplock Courts, the administration of justice, security arrangements – because ultimately these issues will continue to be addressed within the framework of the new institutional arrangements created by it.

These institutions will continue to exist: The forum for discussion will remain intact even if the issues discussed there are not adequately resolved.

That is not to say that there are no yardsticks for measuring the efficacy of the Agreement. The processes it has set in motion have created a political environment that will either facilitate or further hinder political dialogue between the two communities within Northern Ireland. If, at the end of these processes, dialogue is less possible than in the past, then the Anglo-Irish Agreement will have failed: These processes will not have created an environment conducive to political bridge-building. The following are the main elements of these processes which have yet to fully resolve themselves.

The SDLP

The Agreement calls for many of the functions of the Conference to be transferred to a power-sharing government in Northern Ireland whenever the two communities agree on a form of governance. The assumption here was that the SDLP wanted power sharing and believed it could work. However, the SDLP has since made it clear that it has "no ideological commitment to devolution."[14] Moreover, even though the Agreement has been in operation for several years, there is still no indication that the SDLP has any real idea of what power-sharing arrangements it might find acceptable in terms of the powers and functions it would be prepared to assume, the responsibilities it would be required to share, and the tradeoffs it would be called on to make – in the form of a lesser involvement on the part of the South, a diminution in the authority of the Conference, and the possible removal of the Secretariat, with its complement of Irish civil servants, from Belfast.

The SDLP, therefore, has to settle on an agenda that spells out what it wants and what it will settle for (in terms of participation in the governance of Northern Ireland *vis-a-vis* its aspiration to Irish unity) and develop a policy that balances its requirements for power sharing with its commitment to Irish unity – and the expression of that commitment in the form of the Irish Dimension. To date – other than Seamus Mallon, SDLP deputy leader, saying that the new structure in Northern Ireland would have to have real power, that "it would have to negotiate its fiscal relationship with Britain" and "decide on the whole area of law and security", that the structure, "[would be] a much different type of structure than what was known as devolution" and "much more far-reaching" – the SDLP has been largely silent on the question. For both Unionists and Nationalists, Mallon argues, the word 'devolution' is "insulting and demeaning of the position of Northern Ireland"[15] and the process it suggests is both inappropriate and probably unworkable.

> The accepted meaning of the word here, [he says] is that Northern Ireland people would be given whatever powers and responsibilities the British government decided they would give them and would withhold those that they choose to withhold. The structures of the administrative process in the North of Ireland should be agreed to by the parties in the North and they should have the political support of the parties in the Republic, as expressed through a referendum [in the South] on the same day as a referendum would be put to the people in the North of Ireland. It would be the Irish people exercising self-determination as expressed through their agreement, rather than something which would be decided for them by a British Parliament or a British government.

Would the British government be a participant in these talks? "At some stage, [says Mallon] they would become a part of the process. But we would see the initial discussions as being between the Unionists and the government of the Republic of Ireland." Would the new arrangements require legislative change in the British Parliament? They would, says Mallon. Would this involve constitutional change? They may or may not, he says.

The SDLP's impact in recent years, whether convincing the political parties in the South to participate in the New Ireland Forum or being partly instrumental in persuading the two governments to engage in the talks that led to the Anglo-Irish Agreement, has been mainly passive-aggressive. Both of these initiatives were attempts, in one way or another, to shore up constitutional nationalism (i.e., the SDLP) in the North. Thus, to a considerable extent, the SDLP's successes have been the product of the efforts of others in circumstances in which the process itself was more important than the outcome.

However, if and when the Unionists ever make it to the negotiating table, the SDLP will have to deal in terms of outcomes rather than processes, a situation that will call for the kind of policy debate the SDLP has avoided in recent years, and one that it may not be able to withstand, given the many hues of green – united only by the opposition to the violence of militant Republicanism – that come under its broad umbrella. And so, for the SDLP, too, the costs of not talking have been greater than the benefits of talking. It may simply allow things to stand (the preferred behavior of the passive-aggressive) so that the Conference institutionalizes itself in the form of a *de facto* joint authority – an administrative solution to their quandary that would embrace elements of option three of the New Ireland Forum Report.

In the course of talks with Sinn Fein during 1988 "to explore whether there could be agreement on an overall Nationalist political strategy for justice and peace",[16] the SDLP outlined its thinking: "The Irish people as a whole [had] the right to self-determination; the Irish people should be defined as those people domiciled on the island of Ireland;[17] the Irish people were divided on how to exercise the right to self-determination."[18] Unionists, it argued, have two vetoes. "They [have] a natural veto since they live on the island and since their agreement [is] essential if Irish unity [is] to be achieved." And they also have "a [historical] veto on British policy towards Ireland, a veto to which they had no right whatsoever. That veto was exercised in that British policy denied Irish unity. Up to now, successive British governments had been pro-Union. Now, however, they are neutral in that they are saying, without taking a position themselves, that Irish unity is a matter for those who want it persuading those who do not."[19]

Hence, the cornerstone of the SDLP's policy is Article 1(c) of the Agreement, which declares that "if in the future the majority of the people of Northern Ireland clearly wish for and formally consent to a united Ireland, [the two governments] will introduce and support in their respective legislatures legislation to give effect to that wish." Says Hume:

> [This Article] is an implicit declaration by the British that they have no interest of their own in staying in Ireland. That's a shift in the British position ... In short, the British government is neutral in that it is no longer pro-Union. There is nothing, therefore, to stop the British government from becoming pro-Irish unity in their policies.[20] [The SDLP's] task is to persuade [the British] to go in that direction and to use all their considerable influences and resources to persuade the Unionist people that their best interests are served by a new Ireland, in which Unionist interests are accommodated to their own satisfaction and in which there is a new relationship with Britain.[21]

In the SDLP's view, the best way forward, since "*politically* the positions of Sinn Fein and [the SDLP] [are] not unduly removed from each other and are bridgeable",[22] would be "to attempt to create a conference table, convened by an Irish government, at which all parties in the North with an electoral mandate would attend. The purpose of such a conference would be to try to reach agreement on the exercise of self-determination in Ireland. It would be understood that if this conference were to happen, the IRA would have ceased its campaign. It would also be understood in advance that if such a conference were to reach agreement, it would be endorsed by the British government." If Unionists refused to participate in such a conference, then Sinn Fein, the Irish government, and "other Nationalist representatives" should participate "in preparing a peaceful and comprehensive approach on self-determination in Ireland."[23]

Hume argues (once more putting the SDLP in a passive-aggressive mode) that Unionists must address the key Nationalist-Unionist relationship:

> There are three sets of relationships. There is one in the North, there's the one between Unionists and the rest of the island, and there's the British-Irish. But the central relationship, the most fundamental one, and the one that goes to the heart of the problem is the Unionist relationship – or the lack of it – with the rest of the island, or in more clear terms, the Unionist distrust of the rest of the island. Because that relationship has prevented anything from working.[24] ... Until that relationship is resolved, nothing will be stable or lasting.[25]

The next step, therefore, which should precede interparty talks in the North, "has got to be the Unionists entering into dialogue with the rest of the people of the island." That would take time, but since it is the essential next step, "all the resources of both governments should be used – all our powers of persuasion and everything else – to bring about a situation where the Unionists enter into a dialogue with the rest of the people of Ireland on how we share the island."[26] Talks between the SDLP and Unionists are not necessary before you get talks between the

Unionists and the rest of the people of the island; but, says Hume, "we're willing to talk to Unionists at any stage." "We would be willing to talk to them about a solution," says Seamus Mallon. "We see the means of getting that solution [as being through] their dialogue with Dublin. We would be using any discussions we had with them to promote and explain our analysis of the situation. And to persuade them of the need for proper types of dialogue and negotiations." Would the SDLP use a conference or dialogue between themselves and the Unionists to explore whether they could come up with a power-sharing agreement? No, says Hume: "I'm pointing out that every time we've tried to do that in the past, it failed. And I'm drawing conclusions from that failure. What I'm saying is, Let's discuss all the relationships that are involved – and particularly the central one."

Talks purely within a Northern Ireland framework would be futile. "Because to do so," says Mallon, "would be simply to deal only with one part of the problem. The problem is much more fundamental than that, and to ignore what we would say is the most fundamental part of the problem, would be very bad tactics."

Accordingly, for all these reasons, Unionist proposals for talks among the constitutional parties in Northern Ireland, convened by the Secretary of State, would be unproductive.

What the Unionists are saying [says Mallon] is that talks are held in the North of Ireland, essentially initiated and stage-managed by the British government. That agreement would be reached and then discussion held with the Republic. That we would not see as the proper way to go, because the whole of Ireland is part of this problem and unless you get, as we are looking for, the type of agreement which would accommodate everybody in this island, then it doesn't have that real political or moral authority which is required.

Accordingly, Hume would like to see "Unionists take the bull by the horns and go to Dublin saying, 'We're here, you tell us how our agreement is required as to how we share this island.'"[27] To safeguard Unionist interests and to underwrite the understanding they might reach with Dublin, "Unionists should get an agreement from the rest of the island that any agreement reached on how we share the island to our mutual satisfaction should be endorsed, North and South, on the same day by a referendum, and a majority in each would be required. If a majority in either says 'No,' it would not be on." What he is looking for is an agreement "that would transcend in importance any previous agreement ever made."

But what if Unionists insist that under Article One of the Agreement their consent for a change in their status simply isn't there and that that is the abiding reality Nationalists must acknowledge? And what if they demand that Nationalists bargain from that reality? "Because there's a problem there," says Hume, "from that reality of human relationships which has never been resolved. And because there is no peace or stability in Northern Ireland. And you either want to solve the problem or you don't. And you either take the opportunity of settling our relationships now or become a backwater – and a very ugly, ugly backwater at that." Put another way, Unionists should come to their senses. "They are not just semi-detached but they are clinging in their loyalism to something that patently doesn't want them," says Mallon. "Britain has made it clear to them they are dispensable." He is "surprised that it has taken Unionists so long to find out that their real future lies in this island, in their relationship to us and their relationship with the Republic of Ireland, and not with a British government which treats them as 'paddies' as they treat all of us."

The British guarantee of Northern Ireland's constitutional

position as part of the U.K., which so troubled Hume in 1981 and is reaffirmed in Article One of the Anglo-Irish Agreement, has mysteriously evaporated. No longer is it "a sectarian guarantee ... set up on the basis of a sectarian headcount" trapping the Unionists into "perpetual sectarianism."[28] Rather, in its place there is now a "natural veto," since "Unionists' agreement is essential if Irish unity is to be achieved",[29] as if the labeling of unpalatable realities in new ways eliminates the realities themselves. "The SDLP," it says in another policy document, "does not accept that the British position as stated in Article One of the Anglo-Irish Agreement gives a veto to the Unionists on Irish unity. The British government has no right to do so and it is not the British position that gives a veto to any section of the people of Ireland."[30]

For the SDLP, it is a matter of alchemy. The guarantee simply disappears into the black hole of "natural vetoes". The veto the Unionists have on a united Ireland is not a veto bestowed by the British who have no right to do so but a veto conveyed by their numbers and the force of logic – a position the Unionists themselves have loudly and insistently and unsuccessfully promulgated for years.[31] Article 1(c) is used to insinuate that the guarantee is no longer ironclad, that it only remains to persuade the British to become pro-Irish unity for an inexorable sequence of events to follow. Unionists do not have the right not to be convinced.

But the British position, while it does not give a veto to a section of the people (i.e., the Protestants), does give a veto to a majority. In practical terms, Mr. Haughey is correct. Article One reinforces the British guarantee by making it part of an internationally-binding agreement, a fact no amount of "natural" vetoes can disguise. Moreover, Article 1(c) only makes explicit what is implicit in the Northern Ireland Constitution Act – that the British government will do with Northern Ireland whatever a majority of people there want it to do. Just as it would be presumptuous to suppose that it would be possible to coerce a million people into a united Ireland against their will, it would be equally presumptuous to deny the wish of a majority to do so – a fact former Northern Ireland minister Nicholas Scott acknowledged in 1982.[32] You could, says Peter Brooke, Secretary of State for Northern Ireland, make the same arguments with regard to Scotland. "If the Scottish Nationalist Party," he says, "[were to receive] in excess of fifty percent of the Parliamentary seats in Scotland and [did] so on the proposition that Scotland should leave the Union, whatever the political party in power at the time would regard that as a demonstration of the Scots' wish to leave the Union."

And so, the SDLP dispenses with the issue. Whether the Unionists have the right to say 'No' to Irish unity is "purely academic". The SDLP is "a party of realistic politicians – not a team of theologians." The reality is that "Unionists possess such a veto."[33] That having been conceded, however, the SDLP moves on to its broader agenda and continues not to address the one practical consequence of accepting the reality which has vexed Nationalist policy on the North since the beginning: What to do?, given the absence of Unionist consent to any change in its constitutional relationship to the U.K. When then Secretary of State for Northern Ireland Tom King said that the Agreement "guaranteed the Union in perpetuity,"[34] the Irish outcry reflected, in part, Irish unwillingness to face what might yet be the uncomforting truth.

But it is the SDLP's understanding of process that distinguishes it from the other parties. The Agreement "is a framework that can be used differently by different people at different times."[35] The SDLP will come to the negotiating table with "no

solutions" in hand. You might even have "a permanent conference table [which] itself would transform the atmosphere in
Ireland." Out of the process, "[something] might emerge which
could be totally different from anything that anybody had
thought of" – or if not a solution, then another process. And the
SDLP's agenda? "If we reach agreement on institutions that give
expression to our new agreement [on political matters]," says
Hume, "then I will rule out nothing."[36]

In short, Hume is still holding to the scenario he outlined in
1982:[37] Encourage Unionist disillusionment with the British;
draw the Unionists to the negotiating table; have them make
their demand for independence or something close to it ("The
logic of their position is," he continues to insist, "'we want to be
independent within the United Kingdom.'"[38]); pin them down
on the almost insuperable problems independence would face:
How impossible it would be to secure the consent of the minority, and how opposed the Dublin government would be. At
which point, all parties "would be locked into negotiations for
the first time."[39] Nationalists would then make a counter-offer:
an autonomous Northern Ireland state within a federal Ireland
and an Anglo-Irish Council providing the institutional link with
Britain, which would provide for British citizenship. An agreement along these lines would then be put to the people of the
North *and* the people of the South in two separate referenda; to
become binding, it would have to be ratified in both jurisdictions.

Voices of Unionism

Despite the fact that the Agreement explicitly states that there
will be no change in the status of Northern Ireland without the

consent of a majority of its people, Unionists believe that the Union – that is, the connection between Northern Ireland and Great Britain dating from 1920 and beyond that to 1801 – is over. They further believe that the Agreement, through the Intergovernmental Conference, gives the Irish government a toe hold in the North. The Conference has a permanent Secretariat, based in Maryfield (on the outskirts of Belfast), comprised of both British and Irish civil servants. The Conference is viewed not as a small co-operative gesture but as a coalition government in embryo. In the Unionists' view, the language in the Agreement requiring "determined efforts [to be made] to resolve differences" means that Dublin gets it way fifty percent of the time. The Conference is seen, therefore, as the first step to an all-Ireland state. "When the British government signed the Anglo-Irish Agreement," says the Rev. Ian Paisley, leader of the Democratic Unionist Party (DUP), "whether Mrs. Thatcher knew it or not, she was signing a document, the eventual outcome of which was a united Ireland."

> I think that the British government said, "Yes, we will go for a united Ireland." The Secretary of State has also said recently that he doesn't believe the IRA can be defeated.[40] Well, if they cannot be defeated, then he must be preparing surrender terms for the British government. So the view of the people would be, 'Yes, the British government is trying to sell us out.' Absolutely.

Peter Robinson, deputy leader of the DUP, goes further. For him, "the Union is already broken. The Anglo-Irish Agreement is a positive step toward Irish reunification and isn't a neutral act at all. It is much more than that. It is an attempt, bit by bit, to move us into the Irish Republic."[41] And thus the continuing Unionist anger: Their options are being defined for them by a British government which has not consulted them and an Irish government which has an illegal territorial claim to their province. And thus the questions, which Robinson says, Unionists have to ask themselves: "Are we wanted in the U.K.? Is our future in the United Kingdom? And if it's not, if Britain isn't prepared to give us satisfactory terms, then we will have to look elsewhere." Britain has lost the trust of Unionists.

For Unionists, he says, the purpose of talks will be to find out "whether there are satisfactory terms of membership that we can have within the U.K. Can we work that out without having to give too much in internal structures or, as far as the relationship with the Irish Republic is concerned, to endanger our position within the Union?" And if they cannot work it out? "Well, then [we] haven't weakened [our] position. You've got your answer, and therefore you know there is no future on that front, and you have to chart your course towards a constitutional alternative. All I [want to] know is where I stand, and to bring it to a head."[42]

But deep as their distrust and dislike of the British go, their distrust and dislike of the Irish go deeper and further, and they unhesitatingly dismiss the suggestion that they should throw in their lot with the rest of the people of the island:

> The gut sense [says Robinson] you would get on the street is that the love of the link with the U.K. is always secondary to the hatred for a link to the Irish Republic, and given a choice, they [Protestants] would tighten their belts and look for some form of negotiated independence, dominion status or whatever it might be, rather than go into any united Ireland structure, whether it's a federal Ireland or a unitary state.[43]

Bob McCartney, founder of the Campaign for Equal Citizenship, agrees with Robinson but for different reasons:

> The prospects of Unionists being persuaded that because the Brits have declared that they don't want them or are said to have declared that they don't want them, that they will align them-

selves with an agreement to go into a united Ireland, is nonsense. Because it ignores totally the effect of the IRA terror. Throughout Northern Ireland, there are thousands of people who have been directly injured, there are tens of thousands of people who are related to people who have died or who have been severely mutilated. To suggest that the Unionist population might be persuaded to give their consent to the achievement of an objective which is the same as the IRA's objective [is absurd].

The guarantee in Article 1(a) of the Agreement that the status of Northern Ireland will not be changed without the consent of the majority of the people is simply a "whitewash":

There were two Agreements [Robinson says] because they couldn't agree on what the status of Northern Ireland was. You had an agreement on the part of the Irish Republic. Their document says "An Agreement Between the Government of Ireland and the Government of Great Britain". The one that was presented to the [British] Prime Minister was "An Agreement between the Government of the United Kingdom of Great Britain and Northern Ireland and the Government of the Republic of Ireland". They couldn't even agree on what the front page should say. So it's hardly much of a guarantee when they [the Irish government] say that the status of Northern Ireland can't be changed without the consent of a majority, if they were already stating on the front page that it is the government of [all] Ireland under their constitution.

The Official Unionist Party is split – some would say hopelessly split – between integrationists and devolutionists. Neither wing trusts the other, and the inability of the party to reconcile the two has resulted in a policy stalemate and the absence of effective leadership. Said the late Harold McCusker, Official Unionist M.P. for the Upper Bann at the time of his death:

> We're incapable of resolving it [the split]. We cannot resolve it short of splitting, or short of tearing [the party] itself apart in the process, which is even worse than splitting. We would rip ourselves apart. We've run away from it and we won't resolve it.[44]

And to add to the paralysis, says Ken Maginnis, Official Unionist M.P. for Fermanagh-South Tyrone, "the DUP is forever shadowing us, ready to capitalize on our mistakes, and they're always ready to claim they're more loyal, more dependable, even though they've got a history of changing their stance."[45] "Neither of them [the Unionist parties] know very clearly," Bob McCartney says, "what they ought to be doing. They are going for the option of doing absolutely nothing."

> They are certainly making no moves whatsoever towards devolution. And the reason for that is clear. At the center of the Anglo-Irish Agreement is a devolution core. It has been used as a bait for the Unionists. You want a devolved government, you can have [one] but it must be with the consent of the SDLP and in accordance with a modality approved by the government of the Republic. What the reassessment of the Unionist position since 1985 has afforded is an understanding that devolution is the badge of difference, that it is the strategy whereby the British government have been trying to get them out of the U.K. It's dawning on an increasing number of Unionists that devolution is the kiss of death ... I think instinctively both Molyneaux and Paisley will have absolutely nothing to do with it [devolution].

Although the electoral pact made between the two Unionist parties in 1985 to ensure the solidarity of their opposition to the Agreement has endured, it shows signs of wear and tear, especially since the status quo has worked to the advantage of the Official Unionists.[4] The re-creation of a Unionist monolith, with the various strands of Unionism papering over their differences, left the Democratic Unionists in an ideological vacuum. "I think one of the greatest disasters for [us]," says Sammy Wilson, the DUP's press officer, "was the very close liaison [with Official Unionists] – almost to the point of being absorbed into the Official Unionist Party – since the signing of the Anglo-Irish Agreement."

> Party members – and supporters – were asking, "What is the difference between ourselves and the Official Unionists? You don't even fight them when it comes to elections. Everything is done almost jointly. There really isn't a difference." As a result, we lost a lot of good members. The party organization and the party profile suffered. And that affected the vote in some areas where well-known activists left the party. The other thing we were not clear enough about was, what our alternative to the Agreement was. And I think a lot of people were staying at home because they felt, "Well, look, you're against the Agreement, but we're not actually too sure how we're going to get the Agreement moved or what we're going to put in its place."

To the outside world, the Unionist campaign, "Ulster Says No", to smash the Agreement – which at best was ill-planned and at worst was simply a primeval response to perceived threat – appeared to collapse in unholy disarray. Nothing worked – not the special by-elections they forced when they resigned their seats in the Westminster Parliament, nor their Day of Action when they called a one-day strike in March 1986 to shut down Northern Ireland, nor the sporadic, disorganized street violence, nor the intimidating power of their parades, nor their withholding of local rates, nor the abstention of their councillors from local government bodies and their M.P.s from Westminster, nor their refusal to talk with British government officials, nor their 400,000 signature petition to the Queen. The British government, with the full backing of the Irish government, made it clear that it would not entertain, under *any* circumstances, the Unionists' demand that the Agreement or the workings of the Conference be officially suspended before they engage in talks with the Nationalists about further governance arrangements in Northern Ireland. The Agreement was simply non-negotiable as a precondition to talks.

But Unionists do not see their campaign against the Agreement as being unsuccessful. Even if they have failed to develop a coherent political response to it, are unable to come to grips with how it has affected their real position within the Union, and are unable to figure out how to get themselves back into the political process without losing both face and credibility, they have nevertheless developed a set of positions which have become more entrenched with the passage of time and now have the sanction of holy writ.

First, Unionists believe that their campaign against the Agreement has been effective; although they may not have broken it, they have made it virtually unworkable. Second, they believe that the base of the support for the Agreement has disappeared. The Haughey government doesn't have the commitment to it the FitzGerald government had, and it hasn't produced the benefits the SDLP thought it would deliver. Third, they believe that the Agreement has damaged Anglo-Irish relations.

Fourth, they believe that opposition to the Agreement has become covert, but that Unionist opposition to it remains as strong as ever. Even though people may not be participating in massive rallies, there is no wavering in attitudes towards it. The decision to abandon street protest was tactical, an acknowledgment of the fact that Unionists were playing for the long haul, that street demonstrations alone would not bring the Agreement down, that their campaign was essentially a war of attrition, and that ultimately the Agreement would collapse under the weight of its own internal inconsistencies. Says John Alderdice, leader of the pro-Agreement Alliance Party:

> Opposition to the Agreement is just as strong. Even among people in my party who would have been supportive of the Agreement, there's a great deal of disenchantment that it hasn't achieved what they had hoped it would achieve. And certainly in the Unionist community, there's actually no more thought of supporting the Agreement than there was the day it was signed. But there's also a feeling that protesting against it is totally futile. But I think it would be entirely wrong for Nationalists to take the view that because people aren't coming out into the streets, that there's any support for the Agreement. There's an acceptance that it's there, and there's also a belief that it's probably of less importance than it was made out to be.

Fifth, Unionists believe that, had they a mind to, they could have brought the Agreement down through violence, but they chose not to follow that option. Sixth, they believe that their opposition to the Agreement has forced the two governments to the realization that there has to be an alternative to the Agreement, if its objectives are ever to be achieved.

Seventh, Unionists across the board disagree with Hume's argument that the Unionists' relationship to the rest of the island is at the core of the conflict, and reject his urgings that Unionists would have to work out their relationship with Dublin before interparty talks in the North would be worthwhile. Says James Molyneaux, leader of the Official Unionists and M.P. for South Antrim:

> That is unlikely to be deterred by time's scale, because that's basic. Unless we have the structures arrived at and mutually agreed to and working in Northern Ireland, then there would be no merit [in talking to Dublin]. In fact, it would be counterproductive to

talk unilaterally to the Prime Minister or any Minister in a foreign government.

Ken Maginnis sees other reasons for Hume's suggestion:

For us to talk with Dublin would be a recognition of some sort of the right of Dublin to speak for the whole island. What John Hume suggests is seen as a ruse: 'Go and speak to Dublin, get Unionists to speak to Dublin', and they are recognizing Dublin's inherent right to speak for the entire island.

For John Taylor, Official Unionist M.P. for Strangford, Hume's emphasis on the Dublin-Unionist discussion "is a one line track" and is put down to Hume's being "a United Irelander ..."

The SDLP's attitude is simply that they're no longer interested in devolution within the United Kingdom. They are more interested in a new relationship between Northern Ireland and the Republic of Ireland and that that should proceed on the basis of talks within the context of the Anglo-Irish Agreement. In all of that, they're going to go nowhere.

Hume, says Martin Smyth, Official Unionist M.P. for South Belfast and Grand Master of the Orange Order, is not interested in devolution. The strategy is obstructionist.

It is he, above all, who has withstood devolution of powers even to local councils, when his own party councillors wanted more power to deal with local issues. He doesn't want devolution and therefore he's using this as a ploy to appear whiter-than-white.

Robinson sees Hume's emphasis on the Unionist and the rest-of-Ireland relationship as a decoy.

The key relationship must always be the relationship between the people living in Northern Ireland. It's in Northern Ireland that we have the problem. Therefore, a solution must come about by a resolution of the differences between those people. When you have sorted out the differences between the people of Northern Ireland, everything else follows automatically from it.

Haughey's invitation to Unionists to come and talk with him and his prediction that they would be surprised at how accommodating they might find him is, says Sammy Wilson, "all part of the general Nationalist strategy."

> Charlie Haughey is not any great supporter of devolution. And that [Haughey's invitation] is part of the game that the SDLP are playing, too. He is making an offer which he knows must be refused, and then he can always say, "Well, we can't move because they refused that offer in the first place." And it ensures that there's not a movement towards some kind of more realistic and more acceptable state of affairs here.

For Robinson, however, there is also a strategic consideration:

> He's asking us to work out our relationship with him. I don't think we can do that. First, because we want to know what the internal structure is, and second, because the internal structure gives us our standing, so that we're not going in almost as wee boys to see what Charlie is going to give us. We're going in almost as equals to work out the relationship we're going to have with him. The only thing he would have a right to talk to us about is the relationship that the Republic of Ireland would have with Northern Ireland.

Suspicion of Hume runs deep. His motives are not only questioned but belittled. Unionists do not trust him, do not believe what he says, and hear only what they believe he really means. For them, his overtures are traps, the language of reconciliation perceived as the language of deviousness designed to conceal real intentions rather than to illuminate the political landscape. "You can't trust John Hume," says Paisley. "For him, it's a united Ireland or nothing."

Thus, Hume's invitation to talks "about an agreement that would transcend in importance any agreement ever made" or "for finding a way to share the island of Ireland" is declined, his words ridiculed. "Hume speaks in 'Humespeak'," says McCartney. "Every Unionist [can provide you with] the code for Humespeak. There are all sorts of phrases, like 'a lasting and just and peaceful settlement in Ireland'. That means a united Ireland." Even John Alderdice finds that Unionists have similar, if less pungently expressed, opinions: "I can say quite clearly how Unionists perceive that [Hume's expressions]," he says. "[They believe] John is trying to put them in a position where they will have to negotiate into a united Ireland. That's certainly how it's perceived, there's absolutely no doubt about that at all." Harold McCusker concurred, but expressed himself more truculently: "The hidden wording within all of [Hume's expressions] is that it's an agreed united Ireland. Or if it's not a united Ireland in a structural sense, a united Ireland in the sense that the Northern province would be acknowledging Dublin in the way, perhaps, that we presently acknowledge London. And I think he is in cuckooland if he believes Unionists are going to do that."

Unionist approaches to an alternative to the Agreement vary; some, especially among those who espouse devolution, are similar to the SDLP's in terms of process, even though they would have different starting points and eventually take different constitutional roads. All acknowledge the three relationships as a frame of reference, all recognize that a comprehensive settlement must address all three relationships, some talk about seeking a devolution of powers that would make a Northern Ireland parliament more than a rubber-stamp for Westminster legislation, and some would call for a redefinition of the constitutional link with Britain.

James Molyneaux, an acknowledged advocate of integration,

calls for the devolution of "real power" to the district councils. These would be "modest powers which couldn't conceivably be contentious in terms of politics or religion, [such as] problems [relating to] the repair of roads, the cleaning and lighting of streets, and the supervision of repairs to housing"; a North-South dimension would be for the government of the Irish Republic and the government of Northern Ireland to work out. "To be good neighbors," however, "you don't interfere in each other's households." The relationship between the two islands "would be a matter for the two sovereign governments." John Taylor espouses legislative devolution: Laws passed at Westminster would be administered by a Northern Ireland Assembly through a committee system based on proportional sharing. "Having a devolved government in Northern Ireland making laws," he says, "would involve having people like Seamus Mallon and Ian Paisley in the same cabinet. It would never work." And what of the SDLP's predictable rejection of such an arrangement? "They don't have a veto, and should they not agree and should it not take place – well, hard luck on them. We're moving towards integration."[5]

Martin Smyth favors a federal relationship between Northern Ireland and the rest of the U.K. Ken Maginnis, one of the leaders of the legislative devolutionist wing of the OUP, presses for "sharing of responsibility", a "new side-by-side relationship with Dublin", and a "carefully redefined relationship within the U.K." Ultimately, Maginnis believes Unionists will settle for "some sort of relationship on an equal footing", although one that would stop well short of a federal Ireland.

Ian Paisley calls for "an Assembly of Ulstermen, answerable to their electorate, working in a thoroughly democratic forum at Stormont and with an executive not appointed by a colonial chief, the Secretary of State, but chosen freely by the Assembly administering our affairs"[46] – a form of legislative devolution that does not appear to provide a role for Nationalists in government. "I want as much power as possible," he says, "[including] security powers"; decisions would be made on a majority vote basis, except "in matters of controversy" where Unionists "would be prepared to look at a weighted majority." Peter Robinson argues that for a settlement to stick, it must address the three relationships, since all are inter-related:

> You cannot work out the relationship that you have with the Irish Republic until you know what structures you have in Northern Ireland that it is to be related to. But at the same time, I think it is unlikely that you will get agreement on that internal structure without the SDLP's knowing what the relationship's going to be with the Irish Republic. And, therefore, the process might have to be in tandem – the negotiations internally, and the negotiations as to the relationship with the Irish Republic. And it could well be that Unionists might play a role in the process of negotiating with the Irish Republic rather than simply leaving it to the British government to do. Pragmatically, you will not get agreement on an internal structure unless the minority knows what setting it's going to be in.

And the manner in which that could happen?

> It would be absurd to suggest that we are going to be able to resolve our problems by looking at any one of three relationships and settling it, because they are all inter-linked. What we need is a package, and a package will require us to have agreement on all those matters … I believe that the best way forward, if you are getting down to the mechanics of how you do it, is that you set out what those three relationships would be to your satisfaction and to the satisfaction of the SDLP. And once we're reasonably happy what those three relationships would be, then we try and sell our agreement to other parties to it.

The new arrangements would involve a modification of the Unionist relationship with Britain:

> My view is that the relationship we have with the rest of the U.K. has been altered considerably by the Anglo-Irish Agreement. And, therefore, if we are to have a new British-Irish Agreement, it seems that that relationship will be redefined.

But the Unionists have no strategic approach; their own passive-aggressiveness and a propensity to continue to do nothing are still the cornerstones of their policy. They have not worked out in any systematic way what they want and what they will settle for. Maginnis:

> We're not at that particular point [because] we've never been standing at the negotiating door. There has always been something to keep us back. There have been some constraints on us. Until people believe we're coming to the stage where negotiations will take place, we're not going to concentrate our minds on what we want to achieve within those negotiations. We're much more concerned about what is happening under the terms of the Anglo-Irish Agreement and concentrating our attention on how we can frustrate anything that the Anglo-Irish Agreement might come up with.

Unionists, the late Harold McCusker said, are "leaderless", "rudderless", and "don't really know where they're going or what they're doing", that "after twenty years of this, we are punch drunk. We're a very small community. We're on the defensive now and all we can actually do is counterpunch. I don't believe there are any clearly defined Unionist policies, other than obstruction and pigheadedness."

Robinson, however, sees the Unionist lethargy as part of a more pervasive malaise: the absence of a coherent, clearly understandable, well-articulated goal.

The Nationalist community has a clear and identifiable goal. Whatever policy the SDLP pursues or whatever tactics the IRA pursue, it's aimed at moving them toward that. Unionists have discovered that while the basic tenet of Unionism is to maintain the link between Great Britain and Northern Ireland, it isn't something they can hold or attain themselves. Their goal is one that can be reached only by the grace and favor of someone else, and no matter how much they wanted it, no matter how many people voted for it, no matter how much the community might yearn for it and might be prepared to pay a price for it, they still can't get it unless the British government itself and the British people whom it represents were to have a marriage, if you like, that was acceptable to them. [So the question becomes] if you can't achieve a union that is satisfactory, what sort of relationship can you have on your own with Great Britain and with the Republic of Ireland? It isn't the Unionists who are calling the tune. Unionists are left to react to events because they haven't got an attainable goal. The only time you have an attainable goal is when you set your sights on something you can achieve by your own power and not be dependent on the British government and the crumbs that come from their table. What we want we can only have on the terms that somebody else gives us.[47]

People, however, don't want to believe that the British government is going to withdraw. "They're living in a fool's paradise," says Robinson. "The signs of withdrawal – politically under the Anglo-Irish Agreement – and the signs of withdrawal on the security front – where the British government won't just take necessary measures – are all there."

It is this unwillingness to face up to this reality of their situation that is perhaps Unionists' greatest failing.

Instead of recognizing where they are and plotting a course for themselves from there, [says Robinson] they won't come to terms with the fact that they are where they are and are still trying to get back to where they used to be. When your policies are on that basis and you're not accepting the position you're in, your reactions are wrong and the steps that you take are wrong and what you're really left with is the hope that some incident or series of incidents or occurrences will change the political map. What they're hoping for is that something [will happen] in the future that will stop them from making unpalatable decisions themselves. If we wait for divine intervention, if we wait for something to happen, we'll just drift further.[48]

Maginnis detects a similar disposition to procrastinate in his own party, an unconscious hope for some catastrophic quarrel between London and Dublin, perhaps, that will damage the Agreement beyond repair and allow Unionists to vent their "I told you so" smugness. But it is also a waiting born of fear, the fear that events are beyond their control, that they have lost in some intangible way, difficult to identify with specificity, yet, nevertheless, overwhelming in its angst.

You'll hear my party saying [he says], "After a week or two, when we see what's in the Queen's speech, we'll make a decision", "After we get by the commemoration of the signing of the Agreement, we'll see what's happening." Well, nothing will happen until after Christmas, and then there's that tendency always to sort of half promise that in two or three weeks or two or three months, if you hold on, something will change.

And hence the need for talks becomes increasingly compelling because, Robinson says, "it becomes more and more difficult to change things the longer they are in the statute book." In short, Nationalists are winning:

Go out and speak to anybody … In their honest moments the vast majority of the Unionist community will say the IRA is winning … I think they are winning, and I would be arguing with historical facts if I was to suggest that Unionists weren't losing ground

day by day … That's what I object to, that's why I want to change
the situation, and that's why I get so frustrated when things are
allowed to drift. We keep handing it to our enemies and they get
stronger and we get weaker in these circumstances.[49]

Without an alternative to the Agreement, which both Nationalists and Unionists can agree on, the outlook for the future is
bleak. Says Robinson:

There is no political hope for anybody. If you haven't got a seat at
Westminster, there are no opportunities available to you. The
height of your aspirations is local government. But it isn't just in
the political sphere that depression has set in. I've never spoken
to so many people who are saying they are looking for a job
outside the country. Policemen I've spoken to saying, "If we were
even fighting for a draw, that would be alright." People don't
believe the commitment is there to save the country. They just see
continued violence, and that takes young people not just out of
politics but out of the country. To have any hope, this country
must have at least the hope of ending violence. It isn't there.[50]

Thus the Unionist position: The Agreement has failed and it
is up to the two governments to admit their failure, suspend the
workings of it, and give the constitutional parties some time to
come up with an alternative that would address, to the satisfaction of all, the three key relationships. And if the interparty talks
fail, the two governments could simply re-impose the Agreement. Suspending the Agreement's workings for a specified
period would, said McCusker, put the Unionists on "a very
sticky wicket if they were put in a situation where they were
called on to produce an alternative to the Agreement and
couldn't."

Reality is viewed through a lens that transforms it into a
vindication of their assumed positions, justifies inaction, and

boosts self-esteem. They have assumed a posture of virtuous powerlessness. "There is nothing we can do," says John Taylor.

> It's very easy to make that charge [of their having a "Do Nothing" policy] against us, but what is there we can do? Nothing. The Anglo-Irish Agreement is an agreement between two sovereign governments, and we are not a sovereign government nor a sovereign people. We can simply sit back and let them make a fool of themselves. We can't do anything about it.

They have rationalized their way out of their predicament; their insistence that the Agreement has failed and that the failure is due, in large measure, to the effectiveness of their campaign against it helps them to excuse their own paralysis. Their opposition, they would assert, is principled: They will not resort to actions that will increase sectarian tensions or lead to violence. They are, therefore, "prepared to sit back and wait for events to prove them right." Says Maginnis, "The Agreement can never work. [And the two governments know it.] But their attitude is one of, 'To hell with peace, stability, and reconciliation. Let's maintain the Agreement. If we don't, the Unionists will have their tails up and we don't ever want Unionists to have their tails up.'" Inertia drives the engine of change.

Furthermore, Unionist perceptions that the Union with Britain has been breached in some fundamental sense has undermined one component of their identity – their Britishness. Increasingly, they refer to the Secretary of State for Northern Ireland as a 'proconsul', a dictatorial overlord of sorts who rules over them without regard to their wishes or needs. And increasingly, they refer to Northern Ireland as being a colony, with themselves as the oppressed and hapless natives trying to break free of British neo-colonialism but afraid that freedom may leave them more vulnerable to the designs of another state: the Irish state on their borders – less powerful, perhaps, but potentially far more threatening. "The Protestant community in Northern Ireland," said McCusker, "now sees itself as Ulster people in a way in which it [previously] didn't. For the younger generation, there's less of a sense of British identity." It is a trend that will continue, he says, to the point where you will have, perhaps, "a million people in Northern Ireland developing their separate sense of historical and cultural identity, and demanding that those things be recognized and respected and accorded whatever is accorded to other minority groups in Europe."

Protestant perceptions that the Union with Britain has been breached strengthens another component of their identity – their Protestantism. This, in turn, aggravates the enduring tensions within Unionism itself: between those whose primary interest lies in maintaining the connection with Britain, no matter how unsatisfactory that relationship may be, and those whose primary concern lies not in becoming part of an all-Ireland state. "The Republic hasn't changed one iota [in the last seven years]," McCusker charged. "My freedoms and liberties would be just as threatened today as my predecessors' were seventy years ago."

There are some indications, however, that Unionists are coming to grips with the new realities. "Whether we like it or not," says Wilson, "we're going to have to work within Northern Ireland with opposition parties. Being locked outside the door, since the signing of the Agreement, has brought home to many Unionists just how cold and lonely and frustrating it is to be excluded totally from any say in running your own affairs." Accordingly, says Robinson, "Unionists are making it clear that they're willing to have an agreement with other parties in Ireland as to how Northern Ireland should be administered. They're willing to work out the relationship between Northern Ireland and the

Irish Republic. They're willing to put down how [individual and communal] rights can be protected."

They have lost their self-confidence, their assertions of triumphalism reduced to pro-forma incantations. The Union that Protestants cherish has little to do with the *de jure* relationship between Northern Ireland and Great Britain. It is something more intangible, almost a spiritual thing, more a sense of communion, of belonging, even of being a special member of the United Kingdom family which cherishes all its children equally, than a set of reciprocal obligations and responsibilities. The Union has a metaphysical meaning; it is a symbolic statement of shared values that transcends the *de facto* arrangements the Union stands for. The Agreement severed this special bond. "There's the state of the Union as defined in statute," said McCusker. "Then there's the state of the Union – which is the important state of the Union – which is as it is in people's mind. And if you ask Unionists in Northern Ireland what's the state of the Union, [the majority] will say, 'Bloody awful.'"

And while he acknowledged that the Agreement may not really harm Unionists' interests in political terms, that, he said, is to miss the point:

It was never the practical implications of the Agreement which concerned people like myself. It was the psychological implications. It was the major concession made to Dublin that the Union was a very conditional matter, that Northern Ireland wasn't really a part of the United Kingdom, that it was only a part as long as people sort of went along with it. And as soon as a majority of one didn't want it, the British government would rush to change.

They see themselves as the victims, the unrepresented, the community without a voice or a voice to speak on their behalf. "Part of the theory behind the Agreement," said McCusker, "is that, while the Irish government is there as a surrogate for the minority community in Northern Ireland and their representatives, the British government is there as surrogates for the majority. The British government is not a surrogate for the majority community in Northern Ireland. In fact, invariably, over the last twenty years, it's been hostile to everything we aspire to."

And so, they compose themselves: Abandoned by the British, as they would have it – in all but the most circumscribed legal sense – they harbor dark thoughts of rebellion but draw back at the brink, not quite yet, or, indeed, not, perhaps, ever prepared to let "natural forces" have their way. "We don't have the guts," said McCusker, "to stand up and say, 'We're not going to be governed in a way that we don't want to be governed. We're not prepared to be treated as serfs.' Or, we have been prepared to say it, but we've not been prepared to do anything about it. And protest without effective action is not protest." But this begs the question: Effective action for what?

In the Official Unionist Party, Molyneaux's minimalist "Do Nothing" politics is as much a product of strategy as of paralysis, and to the degree that it advances integration, it suits his purposes admirably. The absence of talks on devolution is "playing into the hands of the integrationists," says John Taylor. "If Dublin and London don't seize the opportunity [for talks], Unionists will just sit tight as they've been doing for ten years and Northern Ireland will slowly become more integrated into the U.K."

Mr. Molyneaux is a cautious man, bound by the precedents of proper procedures. And since "it is an accepted convention that leaders of opposition parties [such as Neil Kinnock and himself] do not negotiate with foreign countries behind the back of [their] own government", it would be *improper* for him to talk with

Haughey – it would be a breach "of civilized convention". In the same vein, it seems to him improper that the Anglo-Irish Agreement should extend only to Northern Ireland. "It really ought to extend," he says, "to the whole of the United Kingdom and the whole of the Irish Republic. They'll get three times as many Irish citizens living and working in England as they have in Northern Ireland who would want to be Irish citizens and hold Irish passports." He has, he says, "made a study of Irish papers in the Birmingham and London areas" and read of the "sense of grievance felt by the Irish community in terms of job and housing and education discrimination." To him it makes sense "if the Irish government is to be given protective power status [for] that status [to] extend to the whole of the United Kingdom." In other words, if an Anglo-Irish Agreement were to make no distinction between the role of the Irish government in regard to Irish nationals in Northern Ireland and the rest of the United Kingdom, Molyneaux could support it because it would require the Irish government to implicitly recognize Northern Ireland as being an *integral* part of the United Kingdom.

"The onus is not on us," says Molyneaux, "to prove that the Agreement hasn't worked. The onus is on its designers to show that it has worked – and that they have consistently failed to do." The gulf between Catholics and Protestants in Northern Ireland "is deeper than before the Agreement was signed." Nationalists who liked to think that Unionists had backed down when the British government had stood up to the threat of its violence were "not of a particularly generous spirit."

> On the evening of the Day of Action on 3 March 1986, [he says] I condemned the whole thing root and branch and made it quite clear that they would never be given another opportunity to engage in such activity. That's why the paramilitaries in Northern Ireland, to put it plainly, hate my guts.

He opposes mandated power sharing – "It is unworkable" – or other arrangements that would call for "a permanent all-time coalition" because it would "render elections null and void and unnecessary and redundant". Voluntary power sharing, however, is another matter: "It would take account of election results and [we could] then see what collection of parties could be brought together in a coalition." "[It would be] something voluntarily done by all parties in consultation. It wouldn't be power sharing laid down by statute, saying in advance of elections – no matter what the result of those elections – that you weren't going to alter [a predetermined] proportionality." "Unionists would not contemplate participating in any structure which would be under the supervision of the Anglo-Irish Conference. That [is] one [matter] which is absolutely agreed to by everybody in [the Official Unionist Party] and the Democratic Unionist Party." Above all, he has a determined resolve to ensure that "Northern Ireland will remain an integral part of the United Kingdom" and for that purpose "to have as much power restored to the representatives of the people of Northern Ireland in a devolved structure as is possible in a workable form."

In the Democratic Unionist Party, Ian Paisley is a prisoner of Paisleyism. Having dominated Unionist politics for close to twenty years and climbed to his position of preeminence over the political carcasses of the Unionist leaders he destroyed when they tried to reach an accommodation with the Nationalists, he now finds himself facing the step that might lead him to join them on the refuse heap of Unionist has-beens.

"Hume," he says, "will not talk and doesn't want to talk and every time he is forced into a position to have talks, he backs away. He does not want talks within Northern Ireland." "Hume," he says, "has handed over his responsibility to speak for the Nationalist people to the Dublin government." Accordingly, "it's far better for the people who want a united Ireland to have the sort of vacuum we have at the moment, where all the matters that come before Westminster are decided at the Anglo-Irish Conference."

The obstacles to talks: "There must be a recognition that the Anglo-Irish Agreement has failed, [and] the Agreement would have to cease to be implemented during the time of negotiations and the Secretariat that serves it would have to be closed." Otherwise, "Unionists would not be equal. They would sit in the cage of the Anglo-Irish Agreement with a gun at their heads." The electoral pact between the two Unionist parties "consists of a piece of paper signed by Ian Paisley and Jim Molyneaux, vowing that we're absolutely opposed to the Anglo-Irish Agreement and that neither party will negotiate uni-laterally." Unionists "don't want talks with John Hume." They want talks with "the British government and the constitutional parties." Furthermore, "the British government would have to be in the chair at such talks. It's them that are going to make the final decision, not John Hume." Hume, he thinks, "can't deliver, and that's why he [doesn't] want talks, because he knows he can't deliver."

As regards the state of the Union: "Let us be absolutely clear about this," he says. "If tomorrow morning the British govern-ment came out with a declaration that [said] 'We don't want you', this country would vote by a very large margin that we're not going into a united Ireland. If there was any attempt to force this province into a united Ireland, all hell would be let loose, and what you've seen heretofore would only be a picnic." And even though he has never been an advocate of an independent Ulster ("It's not a practical proposition."), in these circumstances "that's what we would do [and] the British government would be responsible [for the consequences]." Neither the British government nor Europe can afford to have "a wilderness" on their doorsteps.

And why would Haughey want to talk with Unionists? "It's a very simple thing," he says.

> Haughey wants me at the table to have a photograph in all the world's papers so that Haughey can say "At long last, I have been the mighty man who has brought the Unionists to the table." That's what he wants. [It's] a meaningless charade. I could only talk to Dublin when we have the basis of a devolved administration here in Northern Ireland and when I would be negotiating on the part of Northern Ireland for matters of mutual interest which the Assembly in Northern Ireland agreed we should talk to Dublin about.

There would be no talk about the nature of the relationship between North and South: "We are part of the United Kingdom and we're not going to have [them] interfering with our affairs." And the matters of mutual interest?: "Agriculture, the Border, development matters that each part of Ireland has a stake in. [There would be no question] of entering into negotiations to form some new relationship."

If Dublin and London wish to believe that opposition to the Anglo-Irish Agreement has subsided, "let them think it," he says. "They are living in a fool's paradise. And if they want to live in a fool's paradise and go over the precipice, that's their business." The main achievement of Unionism since the signing of the Agreement is "to have stayed together and to have kept united against the Anglo-Irish Agreement." And the Unionist strategy?: "To keep the pressure up. The pressures are now so severe that they are now all calling for us to speak."

> There was a time [he says] when they didn't want to speak to us. There was a time I read articles in the paper, "Paisley can walk it

alone and go into the wilderness forever. Nobody wants to speak to him. He's a back number. Jim Molyneaux is a back number. The steam is out of all opposition. We have won the day. You better agree, you better cut your losses," and so on. Well, if that's so, let them carry on.

The Protestant people will resist any attempt to have others decide matters for them: "John Hume [is saying] 'We've got you Unionists on a hook, we've got you in a place we've never got you before, we succeeded in hooking the British government into it, and by golly, we're going to give you the boot.' And I'm saying on behalf of the Protestant people, 'We're not taking the boot.'" "The long-suffering Protestant population could break," he says. "You can't jack-boot people year after year and malign them and attack them and think they'll not turn. Even a worm at the end of the day will turn."

Rhetoric aside, the fact remains that before Unionists can engage in *substantive* talks with Nationalists about future political arrangements for the North, they must decide what their relationship to Britain means to them and what the continuing form and extent of that relationship is to be. "It seems to me," says Sammy Wilson, "[that the British are saying] 'Look, the relationship's breaking down. We're going to have to get a divorce. But we'll not give you that divorce until we've arranged another marriage for you.' That's one reason why people say 'Well, if that is our option, we're going to stick it out and work at the present relationship and try and improve it rather than go for the divorce.'"

It has been a long, painful, and ultimately may even be an unsatisfying process, but until they resolve these questions, talks with Catholics are not likely to achieve anything substantive. The Agreement, therefore, is a catalyst, which by requiring Unionists to redefine their relationship to Britain, will, by necessity, require them to redefine their relationship to the rest of Ireland. Meanwhile, however, Unionists struggle on, not yet willing to come to terms with the unpalatable options they face: Either to do nothing and watch the Agreement develop stronger institutional hold, or to do something and admit that the Agreement is a fact of life.

For Unionists, perhaps, a Hobson's choice.

Sinn Fein

At first, the Armalite-and-ballot-box strategy succeeded beyond Sinn Fein's wildest expectations. Nothing, it seemed, could go wrong. In 1982 it received thirty-five percent of the Nationalist vote in the Assembly elections and the Eire Nua policy was abandoned. In 1983 its share of the Nationalist vote skyrocketed to forty-three percent in the British general elections and Gerry Adams became President, thus consolidating the Northerners' grip on the movement. In 1985 Sinn Fein candidates elected to local councils took their seats. And in 1986 the electoral battlefield was broadened when the Sinn Fein Ard Fheis (annual conference) voted to abolish abstentionism as it applied to the Dublin Parliament, a *de facto* recognition of the Irish state leading to the inevitable split when the old leadership, Ruairi O'Bradaigh and Daithi O'Conaill – still unwilling to concede the legitimacy of the Twenty-Six County state – walked out and founded Republican Sinn Fein.

The Anglo-Irish Agreement was met with both tempered condemnation and uncertain wariness. Adams denounced it as an attempt "to isolate and draw popular support away from the Republican struggle, while putting a diplomatic veneer on Dublin rule, injecting a credibility into establishment 'Nationalism' so that British rule and the interests it represents can be stabilized in the long-term, and insulating the British from international criticism of their involvement in Irish affairs."[51] But the condemnation was tentative because the uproar the Agreement provoked in the Unionist community was in itself sufficient to ensure support for it among Nationalists, who were convinced that there had to be something substantial in it for them.

In time, the Sinn Fein vote leveled off at one-third of the Nationalist vote. While it was clear that the Agreement had, at least for the short term, blunted the rise of Sinn Fein as a political force, it was also clear that Sinn Fein could command a substantial minority of the Nationalist vote, no matter what. The IRA's campaign, carried out by, at most, 250 activists,[52] became more targeted, requiring a level of violence that would disrupt public and private life and keep the security forces on their toes. In the late 1980s, the violence escalated as if to remind people that the ballot box was always secondary to the armed struggle. But the bombing at Enniskillen,[6] on the 8th of November 1987, which killed eleven Protestants attending Remembrance Day services, brought down on the Republican movement a torrent of condemnation from every side of the political and religious divide. For one brief moment, it appeared that Enniskillen might be a watershed, that the outpouring of grief and outrage might become a catalyst, bringing all the constitutional parties in the North to the table. But the moment passed, and in early 1988, the SDLP rescued Sinn Fein from the political and moral shunning Sinn Fein had been subjected to after Enniskillen when it opened talks with them.

During the talks with the SDLP, Sinn Fein presented its analysis of the conflict. "Given the length to which Britain goes to remain [in Northern Ireland]," it argued, "one can only conclude that it believes it is in its interests to maintain the

IRISH LIBRARY

Union."[53] British government policy "upholds the Unionist political allegiance of a national minority against the national and democratic rights of the majority." Moreover, "when a people are divided in political allegiance, the democratic principle is that majority rights should prevail." While Sinn Fein would concede that Unionists have democratic rights, "these rights do not extend to a veto over the national rights of the Irish people as a whole." "A guarantee of the maintenance of partition in perpetuity leaves Unionists with no reason to seek a consensus."[54]

Britain's actions, one of the Sinn Fein position papers asserted, "totally contradict SDLP claims that Britain somehow is now neutral since the signing of the [Anglo-Irish] Treaty."[55] Decolonization must begin with the British government "repealing the Government of Ireland Act and publicly declaring that the Northern Ireland statelet is no longer part of the United Kingdom." It must further declare "that its military forces and its system of political administration will remain only for as long as it takes to arrange their permanent withdrawal." "A definite date within the lifetime of a British government would be set." Such "an irreversible declaration of intent would minimize any Loyalist backlash." Faced with "a British withdrawal and the removal of partition, a considerable body of Loyalist opinion would accept the wisdom of negotiating for the type of society which would reflect their needs as well as the needs of all the other people in Ireland." Once a society "free of British interference" is established "sectarianism [would] shrivel" and "class politics [would] emerge."[56]

Armed struggle "is a political option,"[57] it is "forced upon the IRA."[58] The SDLP's "bargaining leverage are proof enough that the armed struggle has been beneficial to the political aspirations of the Nationalist community."[59] Since the SDLP "[accepts] the

Hillsborough Agreement," it is now "the linchpin of a British government strategy which seeks to resolve the contradiction of the Northern Ireland state," a strategy "aimed at stabilizing the Six Counties in its own interests by introducing limited or symbolic reforms which attempt to make the northern state more tolerable to a section of the Nationalist community and to international opinion." "Cross-border security cooperation from Dublin actually ensures there is no resolution of the national question."[60] "It is dishonest to argue," the position paper also said, "that Britain's role is that of a neutral peacekeeper," and it accused the SDLP "[of sharing] in a very public way, with the British government, the common aim of destroying the Republican movement."[61] Furthermore, "the public perception engineered by the SDLP that Unionist acceptance of the Hillsborough Agreement [would be the end] of Unionist power and the Unionist veto on the Irish peoples' right to self-determination is a dangerous political illusion."[62]

An all-party conference would only be the best way forward if there was "a prior declaration of intent to withdraw from Ireland by the British government."[63] In the absence of such a declaration, Unionists, assured by the veto confirmed on them by the British government, would feel under no compulsion to move toward a consensus on the means to constructive British disengagement. What, it asked the SDLP, did unity by consent mean? Would the SDLP define what it means by a majority? But the SDLP did not respond.

At the core of the new strategy – "armed struggle in the Six Counties in pursuance of British withdrawal and political struggle throughout the whole thirty-two counties in pursuance of the Republic, breaking out of isolation and becoming politically relevant, [blending] the national struggle with contemporary reality as perceived by the majority of people in the Twenty Six counties" is how *An Phoblacht/Republican News* articulates it[64] – there is a contradiction. The greater the commitment to armed struggle in the North, the less the appeal of Sinn Fein to voters in the South who are being asked to sanction violence. The poorer the performance of Sinn Fein in the South, the more it exposes the IRA's lack of legitimacy. On the one hand, the drive for success at the ballot box creates pressures to subordinate the armed struggle to political pragmatism; on the other hand, lack of success simply reflects the real lack of support for the IRA's campaign of violence. "Without politics you may be able to bomb and shoot a British connection out of existence but you will not bring anything into existence," writes Gerry Adams.[65] But what if the violence makes the politics impossible? What then? In the final analysis, Sinn Fein's identity is inseparable from its relationship with the IRA. Without that relationship, it is little more than a left-leaning, essentially working-class party with a limited constituency and of limited consequence. With that relationship, it exacts an impact on events out of all proportion to popular support for its policies. The power of the movement comes out of the barrel of a gun.

Sinn Fein, however, does not see the Armalite-and-ballot-box strategy as being a failure. "It forced the British government into adopting the Hillsborough Treaty in an effort to counter us," says Morrison, "and despite our electoral fortunes, we still maintain a veto over the entire breadth of manoeuvrability of the SDLP. We can curtail their room, the amount of compromising they can do – we remain a threat."

Moreover, it makes careful distinction between support for the armed struggle and the electoral performance of Sinn Fein, emphasizing that one is not necessarily dependent on the other. "No Sinn Fein person," says Gerry Adams, leader of Sinn Fein, "has ever claimed that a vote for Sinn Fein is a vote for the IRA

... The most that can be said about a vote for Sinn Fein and support for the IRA is that a vote for Sinn Fein is, at the very least, not a vote against the IRA."[66]

Where, then, does the mandate for the armed struggle come from? "The IRA gets its mandate," says Adams, "to fight from the presence of British troops in this country. It doesn't seek an electoral mandate. It comes from the British claim to sovereignty over this part of Ireland."

But what if support for Sinn Fein falls below some threshold level – say five percent – would the Republican movement interpret that as a lack of support for the armed struggle? Adams:

> I just don't see those circumstances. The struggle is very dug in. I think the degree of resistance and the broad tolerance, while it does go up and down, is dug into a point that the British can't erode it. I don't think that anyone, given the nature of the Irish character, given its ambivalence and the folk memory – I don't think there's anyone who could turn around and say that the majority of people do not support the armed struggle. There's a tolerance, there's an ambivalence, there's an ambiguity, there's a wink and a nod – these are all the old effects of our colonial past[67]
> ... The IRA could not have existed for the period it has existed in the occupied area if it didn't have support. You've got majority tolerance among the Nationalist community in the Six Counties.[68]

Insinuations that Sinn Fein was losing electoral ground to the SDLP are misplaced. "I would defy any other party," says Adams, "to fight politically and electorally the way Sinn Fein does and to have the successes we have had in the face of a campaign of moral blackmail. The people of this diocese [West Belfast] were told it was a mortal sin to vote for Sinn Fein."[69]

For seven years Sinn Fein had to "repulse psychological and propaganda attacks from Dublin, London, the Loyalists, the

Orange Order, and the Unionist parties" on its base of support. In contrast, lifelines were thrown to the SDLP, first, "in the form of the New Ireland Forum," and second, "in terms of the Hillsborough Agreement". Furthermore, resources "both financial and otherwise" were channeled to the SDLP from their friends in the U.S.[70]

> If you look at Sinn Fein, [says Adams] [you see] a party mostly made up of working-class people, people with very little formal education and very few professional people involved – an organization which is badly funded and run out of ramshackle buildings, which came together to fight its first election in the early 1980s and has never been able to organize in such a way that would match our potential … Our opponents thought the Sinn Fein vote was going to collapse to four percent or five percent last May [the 1989 local elections] and were quite thunderstruck when it moved only a small percent.[71]

They are not stuck. On the contrary, the struggle was moving on.

> We ended up with a vote [in the Twenty-Six counties in the June 1989 elections] we deserved and it's only by the mundane, tedious, hard work that we can start to reverse it. In the Six Counties, I would defy any political party anywhere in the world faced with the obstacles [we faced] – in terms of censorship, electoral obstacles for our supporters, and all the other obstacles which our supporters labour under – to hold the vote.[7] But what we have done is that we have held our vote. Our vote is 11.4 percent [of the total vote] but we had between thirty and forty percent of the Nationalist vote. That's commendable, so I'm not in the least bit despondent.

Moreover, says Morrison, the rules of the game are constantly being changed to put Sinn Fein at an increasing electoral disadvantage.

We had a whole series of measures introduced to hurt us, to inhibit us, from going in this political direction, from sustaining our support ... There are nine new conditions placed on people standing for elections [since I spoke to you in 1982]. For example, it used to be that ex-prisoners – who would probably make up some of the most talented, most articulate people we have – couldn't stand for election for five years after the date of their conviction. Now they can't stand for elections for five years after their date of release. This is a political move aimed at limiting the pool of potential candidates at Sinn Fein's disposal, particularly at the local government level.

But what has the Republican movement to show after twenty years of struggle? Is it any closer to achieving a united Ireland than it was in 1969? "Twenty years ago," says Adams, "we had a largely apathetic and leaderless Catholic [community]. Now Republicanism is a very important and strong part of the entire equation. It cannot be ignored. No one can look at a resolution to the problem without taking on board the Republican attitude to whatever arrangement is being considered." As regards the ultimate goal of the thirty-two county Republic, "[we] have not progressed towards that in any realistic sense and they will not make any progress towards that until British disengagement brings about a national democracy."[72]

The British are closer now to disengagement than they were twenty years ago. "Twenty years on, the British government is very slowly being brought round to actually being forced to debate the issue [of withdrawal]. The old replies from the British [to explain] their failure of twenty years do not have the same impact on British public opinion [as they used to]. I'm not suggesting that the present government is any closer to withdrawal than, for example, the Wilson government may have been, but what I am saying is that the option of withdrawal is becoming more of an issue."[73]

But where is the evidence of progress? What can the movement point to that would support its claims that progress is being made? It isn't so much of a question of what the movement could claim on its own behalf but of what the British couldn't claim:

> The British have been unable to put a lid upon the situation. Only last week, Brooke publicly admitted that his forces couldn't defeat the IRA, that he will not rule out future talks with Sinn Fein.[74] [Four years after] the Hillsborough Agreement, after the unprecedented coming together of the Dublin government and the English establishment, and the unprecedented military cooperation and the unprecedented harmonization of various laws – all to isolate Sinn Fein and defeat the IRA – the British Minister in charge is saying you can't defeat the IRA and they have to talk to Sinn Fein.[75]

"The timing of Brooke's statement was extraordinary," says Morrison. "Our information is that he said it quite consciously, quite deliberately, in a calculated fashion. Imagine the effect it must have had on the troops out in the street when they realize they are engaged in a campaign they cannot win. So, it's bound to be good for Republican morale."

On the larger question:

> Look at what the British government has done in the last seven-year period – from a 1981 position when Mrs. Thatcher described the hunger strikes as the IRA's "Last Card", to a 1989 position where a Secretary of State – not a former Secretary but one on the job – says, "The IRA can't be militarily defeated." Where has Britain advanced in these last seven years? A guerrilla actually only has to [frustrate] the ability of the government to stabilize the situation in the government's interests. A government to win actually has to show it is winning and the British government cannot demonstrate that.

Sinn Fein unequivocally rejects Hume's assertion that the British are now politically neutral:

> [The SDLP] just don't seem to be analyzing the Brits [says Morrison]. When they turned around and told me the Brits were neutral, I damn near fell through the chair. And then when John Hume was challenged on that, he says to me, "Well, they're politically neutral, but they're not neutral militarily." I just don't know how the SDLP can say the Brits are neutral, given the lengths to which the Brits are prepared to go to maintain their presence in the North – given the things they won't do for the SDLP and the Dublin government.

Adams goes one step further: "I don't think even John [Hume] really believes that [the British are politically neutral]. I think he was put in a situation in the course of those talks [the Sinn Fein/SDLP talks] in which he had to cast about for some position."

But doesn't Article One of the Agreement state that the British will only stay for as long as a majority want them to and that as soon as there is a majority in favour of unity, the British government will pass enabling legislation?

> It's a Catch-22 [says Adams]. They're talking about an artificially impossible mathematical majority. They carve out a piece of territory around a group of citizens, a majority of whom are Unionists. And then they say they will accept the wishes of a majority. The island of Ireland and all its citizens are the unit in which those decision should be made ... It's a flawed position ... If the British are neutral, we said to them [the SDLP] towards the end of the talks – in fact, this is one of the reasons why the talks came to an end – we said to them, "Why doesn't Dublin ask the British government to outline various scenarios towards Irish independence? Because if it's neutral, while it might not be for a united Ireland or an independent Ireland, it certainly wouldn't be against it, and if you really believe it is neutral, prove it." And of course he couldn't do that.

The Anglo-Irish Agreement is a failure: It has delivered on none of the things it had promised. "Our analysis of the [AIA] hasn't changed one iota," says Morrison. "We said at the time that the objective of the British government was to confront the Loyalists in a sense, by stating that the relationship had changed – although, of course, it substantially hasn't changed – and to split the Loyalists, to create an emergent pragmatic leadership which would enter into a power-sharing arrangement, although it may have been called something else, with the SDLP. There's no indication that objective is on its way to being achieved."

Is the SDLP in favor of devolution? "Of course they are," says Adams. "It isn't an impression. It's part of their policy." Would the armed struggle oppose devolution?

> You'd have to put that question specifically to the IRA. Would the SDLP take up a position where it is in support of the RUC and the British army against Republicans? Would the SDLP take up a position where it was responsible for the imprisonment of Republicans? ... The fact of the situation is that the SDLP do favour a Six-County arrangement. They are a partitionist party. And for them to assume any real role in a [Six-County] administration means they ally themselves not just with the upholding of British rule, but with enforcing the implementation of all the structures and penal apparatus in this state.

Isn't calling on the British to made a declaration of intent to withdraw asking them to surrender? Isn't the condition for a cease-fire a demand to surrender? "No," says Adams, "it's calling on the British to come to their senses – one shouldn't confuse sanity with surrender." There are no divisions within the Republican family, no view that the armed struggle has no future. There is, of course, a healthy debate about the use of resources. "For example," says Morrison, "say a person has been in jail for five or ten years and has got interested in Republican politics.

Well, that individual finds that his or her score for getting involved in politics at an electoral level are fairly curtailed [and] would be more likely to reach a conclusion in 1989 than in 1982 that the way forward was through increased military action."

Is Sinn Fein in a stronger or weaker position than it was five years ago? "It's hard to say," says Morrison. "In terms of the Six Counties, I think that organizationally, we're about in the same position. Intellectually and politically, we're in a much stronger position."

And in the Twenty-Six Counties? "We're in a weaker position." The emigration of young people from working class areas has depleted Sinn Fein's natural base of support; censorship restrictions have curbed its growth; they underestimated the obstacles to organizing on a large scale, the sheer amount of work that has to be done to launch a broad-based electoral campaign. Can the South be turned around? "It might well be that the North has to be the engine and that we have to win contests on the basis of our success in the North."

"Personally, I believe that the Twenty-Six Counties, that the Free State, is the key to the overall struggle," Morrison had confidently asserted in 1982.[76] Seven years on, in 1989, that goal is more elusive than ever, and if one were to measure the progress of Sinn Fein on the basis of the headway it had made in the South in the intervening years, it would be found severely wanting.

Sinn Fein, too, of course, can rationalize its setbacks, explain its failures, and convince itself that its way is the only way forward, that if there is a better way of achieving a united Ireland, it is up to those who denounce the IRA to come forward with such a plan. In the Sinn Fein perspective, it has withstood the best efforts of the British government to destroy it and solidified its not inconsiderable base of support in the North, despite political initiatives and deliberately imposed electoral obstacles to undermine it. And while Sinn Fein's support in the North may have leveled off, it will argue that actual support is considerably higher than declared support. There is a "majority tolerance", Adams argues,[77] North and South, among Nationalists for the armed struggle.

The IRA, Sinn Fein maintains, is the catalyst for change, and insofar as the Anglo-Irish Agreement addressed Catholic grievances in some small way, that, too, is attributable to the efforts of the armed struggle. In the South, the emigration of young people had "robbed Sinn Fein"[78] of its natural constituency, and censorship restrictions make it difficult to communicate with the larger public. The mandate for the armed struggle comes from a higher power. There is no question of the people having the right to be wrong on the national question. At no point in the history of Irish resistance have any of those who are lauded as heroes ever looked for a popular mandate for the armed struggle. The mandate for the armed struggle is "a living mandate."[79]

The IRA, Sinn Fein also maintains, are winning because they are not losing, and the British are losing because they are not winning, because increasingly the government is coming to accept that it is in a no-win situation, because support in mainland Britain for a continued British presence in Northern Ireland will ultimately depend on the government being able to show that progress was being made – something it simply can't do. Setbacks are part of the price of a war of attrition. There will be "no cease-fire until the IRA's conditions for one are met",[80] "the mandarins of Whitehall" have "a scenario for British withdrawal packed away in some filing cabinet and one day it will be used."[81] The claims being made about Hillsborough "were increasingly threadbare," says Morrison. The SDLP and the Dublin government can't admit that the Agreement is a failure because "If the SDLP admits that they're wrong, who's right then? It's Republicans. Are the SDLP going to commit political hari-kari?" There is no question of a cease-fire – "no consensus, no momentum, no popular call, no private call, no secret collective meeting" that argues for it.

They have come a long way since 1982. Back then, says Morrison, they were perhaps "a bit overconfident, too excited at our earlier electoral successes and their potential for moving the British in the direction of negotiation." In fact, however, their electoral successes "moved the British government in a reactionary direction." Rather than working to negotiations, the government "very actively, very clearly and ingenuously [came at Sinn Fein] from many different directions." But they have survived, and Republicans have "a seasoned confidence in 1989" and "are a lot wiser" than they were in 1982.

The South

When John Hume was asked in August 1986 whether a Haughey government would abandon or seek to renegotiate the Agreement, he replied confidently that it would do neither. "[A Haughey government] would recognize the extreme danger," he said, "of abandoning the Agreement and thereby reinforcing the Orange card in a massive way because that would be claimed as a major victory by the Loyalist forces."[82] And indeed, when Haughey became Taoiseach in March 1987, he moved from outright opposition to the Agreement and a questioning of whether it had done anything to improve the lot of Nationalists in Northern Ireland to endorsing it, albeit with continuing caveats that progress had been difficult and disappointingly slow. Within a year the mettle of that endorsement was put to severe test.

A string of extraordinary events at the beginning of 1988 brought Anglo-Irish relations to their lowest level in years. The Stalker/Sampson investigation into allegations that the Royal Ulster Constabulary (RUC) had engaged in a shoot-to-kill policy in the early 1980s was completed. However, the British attorney general, Sir Patrick Mayhew, announced in Parliament that the report would not be made public and that eleven senior RUC officers, said to have been named in it for perverting the course of justice, would not be prosecuted, for national security reasons. Dublin, which was not consulted beforehand about these decisions, strongly protested both the decisions and its total exclusion from the process that led to them.

On other fronts, the Court of Appeal rejected the plea by the Birmingham Six, and the House of Lords refused to hear the case. Dublin and London wrangled over extradition. The Home Secretary, Douglas Hurd, took steps to make the Prevention of Terrorism Act permanent.[8] When Aidan McAnespie, a twenty-four-year-old native of Monaghan in the South, was shot dead at a Border checkpoint by a British soldier, the Irish government appointed the deputy commissioner of the Gardai [police] to inquire into the killing rather than use the Intergovernmental Conference to express its concerns. The anger over McAnespie's death was compounded when it was learned that Private Ian Thain, the only British soldier ever convicted of killing a civilian in Northern Ireland, had been released after only twenty-six months of a life sentence for the murder of Thomas Reilly in West Belfast, and had returned to his regiment.

Three unarmed members of the IRA – Sean Savage, Danny McCann and Mairead Farrell, who were on a reconnaissance mission in connection with a bombing operation they were apparently planning – were shot dead by British security forces in Gibraltar, raising new questions about shoot-to-kill policies.

Two off-duty British soldiers were savagely beaten by a Nationalist mob and subsequently shot to death when their car accidentally found itself in the middle of the funeral procession for an IRA volunteer – who was one of three people shot dead days earlier by a Protestant gunman who opened fire on the mourners at the funerals of the three IRA volunteers killed in Gibraltar.

What angered Dublin most was London's obvious disregard for the processes of the Anglo-Irish Agreement. Dublin only learned of what London intended to do in the matter of the Stalker/Sampson report when Mayhew read his statement to the Commons. Dublin was humiliated; Britain, it felt, was clearly in breach of the Agreement.

Its humiliation was compounded by anger at the British decision not to prosecute. In the eyes of Catholic Ireland, the British government appeared to be condoning a shoot-to-kill policy, its decision, "if not quite an official pardon for murder," was at least "an official acknowledgment," the *Irish Times* noted, that "if murder has been at work, the Crown does not want to know about it."[83] Once more, the IRA had been cast in the role of victim; the belief that members of the security forces, with the approval of their superiors, had engaged in a shoot-to-kill policy put the IRA's actions against the security forces in a different context. The question of who was the perpetrator of violence became more complicated, the IRA's actions less obviously "bad."

And again with the Birmingham Six, Catholic Ireland expressed widespread dismay over the verdict. It was not so much that the verdict was unexpected that raised anger as it was the manner in which it was delivered, the tone of the Appeals Court judges, and their total dismissiveness of the testimony of the appeal witnesses. New witnesses were branded "unconvincing liars, embittered, not worthy of belief"; the suggestion of a police conspiracy was "preposterous"; a retrial was ruled out as "an unreal option."[84] To compound matters, Douglas Hurd, the Home Secretary, almost immediately ruled out any question of clemency. "Only a government of the most extreme insensitivity or one bent on the humiliation of a less powerful state would respond as the Home Secretary did," the *Irish Times* bitterly complained.[85]

Once more, the Irish were reminded of their powerlessness,[9] of the fact that, in the final analysis, there was little they could do, that any action on their part that had a retaliatory intent would work to the advantage of the IRA. They were entrapped: The Agreement's sole remedy in cases where one government felt the other to be acting in bad faith is that "determined efforts will be made to resolve differences." But it provides no remedy when determined efforts are less than successful efforts, other than the right each has to call for a review of the Agreement itself. This option is hardly a realistic one; the presence of Irish civil servants in Belfast – the symbolism of the toehold – is too much to give up. For the Irish to admit that the Agreement is a failure, to close Maryfield and call its representatives home, would be to validate the Unionists' contention that their unrelenting opposition to it has paid off: It would make winners of the Unionists.

And thus, again, the Irish dilemma: Constrained, on the one hand not to appear to be a surrogate for the IRA, and on the other, not to appear to be powerless, they struggled, in the shadow of their powerful neighbor, to assert their independence, increasingly more vulnerable to accusations that the Anglo-Irish Agreement was one more example of the Irish being taken in by the Brits. Ultimately, the resolution of disputes is a matter of good will and faith – British good will and Irish faith – and sometimes it appears to the Irish that British good will is in short supply; one has the power, the other, responsibility with no clear-cut mechanisms that allow it to exercise power. "Anglo-Irish relations will never be of a normal type," says Haughey. "They will never be the way they should be between two friendly, neighbouring countries, as long as the problem of Northern Ireland remains unresolved."[86]

"The people believe," Garret FitzGerald said during an interview with the *Independent* in June 1989,[87] "that because there is a Secretary of State for Northern Ireland, there is a Northern Ireland policy. There isn't. The result is that things are done, the cumulative effect of which can be negative, not because of ill will but because of a lack of appreciation of the consequences of the action being taken. To Irish governments, the whole issue is so important that we cannot afford to act negatively, regardless of the consequences."

The success of the Agreement, he says, "depends on the degree of commitment on the British side," and "to the extent that [that] commitment is lacking at any time, we [the Irish government] are vulnerable, because we would have responsibility without power." However, "although we knew all along that that would be the situation, we had to take that risk in order to make progress. We are, of course, at a disadvantage, because we are the non-sovereign part of the relationship."

"It's hard to imagine circumstances," Dick Spring, leader of the Labour Party and Tanaiste [Deputy Prime Minister], says, "where that [closing Maryfield and calling the Irish members of the Secretariat home] would be a worthwhile thing to do." Although there is "a moral obligation on the two governments to try and resolve differences, there aren't any sanctions that one country can apply to another."

No one, perhaps, felt this slighting of the moral obligation more keenly than FitzGerald himself, who maintained during the Dail debate on extradition in 1987 that he had been given assurances during the negotiations leading up to the Agreement that there would be a full review of the administration of justice in Northern Ireland, which he took to mean either three-judge courts or mixed courts. He would, he insinuated, have been reluctant to sign the Agreement without these assurances.

If the British didn't mean a change in the court system, such as mixed courts or three-judge courts, he would later ask, what change in the administration of justice were they thinking of when they agreed to review the system? Moreover, the joint communique that accompanied the Agreement also promised that the armed forces, especially the Ulster Defence Regiment, would, save in the most exceptional circumstances, operate only in support of the civil power; that is, army and UDR patrols would be accompanied by the police. "Our interpretation of what was agreed to," says FitzGerald, "was that that process would occur quickly. The process of maintaining law and order would be an RUC process protected by the armed forces rather than one done by the armed forces." But again, little or nothing happened. The British government protested that it didn't have the resources to implement the arrangement on a wide-scale basis, leaving the FitzGerald government to wonder why, if there were constraints on resources, the British government had promised action in the first place. The Irish government found the British government's explanation "unconvincing". The result was that in both these high visibility areas, the impact of reform in the minority community "was considerably less than it would have been," according to FitzGerald, "if the matters had been handled in the kind of way we had anticipated at the time."

Nonetheless, despite these tensions, misunderstandings, and disagreements, Irish leaders are virtually unanimous in their opinion that the Agreement has improved Anglo-Irish relations. Says FitzGerald: "Anglo-Irish relations have become much more stable so that even though crises and difficulties arise between the two countries frequently, they can now be dealt with in a less and less emotionally charged atmosphere and in a more constructive way than previously." When the review of the workings of the Conference, which the Agreement called for after three years, was completed in May 1989, both Haughey and Thatcher "reaffirmed their [government's] full commitment to all the provisions of the Agreement and to its shared responsibilities and purposes."

Over the years, however, Mr. Haughey remains remarkably consistent in his analysis of the conflict: Northern Ireland is a failed political entity that cannot be resuscitated. Some moments after assuming office in 1987, he called progress under the aegis of the Agreement "difficult and disappointingly limited";[88] in February 1988, at his party's Ard Fheis, he said that Northern Ireland "is not a workable political entity … as it stands at present";[89] and in April 1988, during a visit to the United States, he said that "the conclusion must be that it is the entity of Northern Ireland itself and its constitution that is the problem" and that "no solution is, in fact, possible within its confines".[90]

Just where Mr. Haughey would stand on talks between Unionists and Nationalists that would have as their frame of reference the resuscitation of that entity remains unclear. He has become adroit at avoiding the issue. " … [T]he preconditions for devolution [the cooperation and consent of both traditions within Northern Ireland] do not exist," he told the Dail in November 1989. "There is no enthusiasm for it in any main political grouping in Northern Ireland," devolution could not be "imposed", and "given the existing political realities in the North, it would be a serious mistake for us to tie ourselves exclusively to devolution as necessarily offering the only way forward."[91]

If the IRA were to end their campaign of violence, he envisages a situation in which "the possibility would open up, as it did in the New Ireland Forum, for a broad consensus among Nationalists on how to achieve political stability based on justice. Our efforts ... could then be constructively directed to persuading our Unionist countrymen that their future lay with us in a partnership of equals and in convincing the British government that the future of Ireland could and should be left to all the Irish people to decide for themselves."[92] Mr. Haughey, it appears, feels under no obligation to persuade or convince the SDLP that devolution is the necessary next step, or to suggest that the two governments should perhaps provide leadership in the matter. The absence of consent for devolution is taken at face value. In contrast, the absence of consent among Unionists for unification is not – perhaps that, somehow, can be overcome by the efforts of "a large majority of the Irish people everywhere." In short, the absence of consent means different things in different contexts.

Fianna Fail continues to hew to its all-party constitutional conference line: The best way forward would be for talks between Dublin and Unionists. Dublin, says the Tanaiste (Deputy Prime Minister) Brian Lenihan, "doesn't regard devolution as relevant to the situation." Fianna Fail – and to that extent the government – accepts Hume's analysis that the pivotal relationship is the Unionist and the rest-of-Ireland one, and that the British government is now politically neutral on the Union. And the elements of Fianna Fail's earlier position remain firmly in place. First, Northern Ireland is a failed political entity: "That," says Lenihan, "goes without saying." Second, a conference of all the parties is the only productive way forward: "That is now the focus ... It is a pragmatic way, the only way now of approaching the subject. Otherwise, it's a complete 'hands-off' situation." Third, the only viable option is a unitary Irish state: "That is the ultimate objective."

Unionist opposition to the Agreement has diminished. Lenihan insists that Unionists will admit, off the record, that talks with Dublin are inevitable; their plangent cries that the workings of the Agreement must be suspended are like the "quoting and requoting of holy writ."

What started off with great fanfare four years ago [says Lenihan] is now diminuendo. It's now just being repeated as a matter of rote. There's no reality in it anymore because it's now quite clear that the Agreement is going to stay, that the Conference is going to stay, and that some progress is being made in all sorts of ways. The Unionist perception of the Agreement as being a hindrance to talks is now seen to be withering. Their opposition to it would now be recognized by London and Dublin as being at a stage where it isn't justifiable but an irrelevant stance.

It is still unclear, however, if the SDLP was able to agree on the forms of devolution it would find acceptable, whether Mr. Haughey would regard these arrangements as just one more empty formula to breathe life back into a failed political entity. It might well be that he finds that the aspiration to Irish unity – which is the *raison d'etre* of Fianna Fail, the largest political party on the island of Ireland and the voice of the Irish Nationalist tradition – is better served through his government's holding out for the constitutional conference it wants and its continued, direct advocacy on behalf of Northern Catholics via a strong, vigorous, and increasingly powerful Intergovernmental Conference, rather than through the relegation of the Conference to a secondary position, which devolution envisages. But if this is the case, there is little evidence of it to date. Opposition party leaders frequently chide Haughey for his failure to work the Intergovernmental Conference and for downgrading the personnel who service it.

His differences with Fine Gael on the issue continue to make it difficult if not impossible for a single Nationalist consensus on the North to develop. In his speech to the Fine Gael Ard Fheis in November 1988, Alan Dukes highlighted the differences between his party's commitment to devolution and Mr. Haughey's. "We differ profoundly from Fianna Fail's approach to Northern Ireland," Mr. Dukes told the conference. "We do not believe and never will believe that the two parts of this island can be brought together if the two communities cannot first be united."[93]

And during the Dail debate on Anglo-Irish relations in November 1989, Dukes chastised Haughey. "Since this present Taoiseach took up office in 1987," he said, "I have asked him repeatedly to state his view on devolution. He has repeatedly refused to state any view."[94] Article 4(b) of the Agreement, he argues, states specifically that the Irish government supports the British government's policy of devolution that would command widespread acceptance. He called on the government "to work with the British government and with the constitutional parties in Northern Ireland to achieve it" [devolution] on the grounds that "the initiative can be taken by the two governments and only by the two governments."[95]

Haughey's advocacy of a unitary Irish state as being the preferred option of the New Ireland Forum, Dukes contends, has led Haughey into a political *cul-de-sac*.

> The difficulty with that [Haughey's position] is that there is no practical sense, that I can see, in which a unitary state is going to be achieved by agreement, in the foreseeable future. It's an unrealistic objective to set. Part of Fianna Fail's problem is that even though they may know the unreality of that, they're afraid to say anything different in case they might be pilloried by their supporters for settling for less than the ideal. That has trapped them into a basically untenable position.

The refusal of the government to take practical steps to show its commitment to devolution contributes to the stalemate.

First of all, they should say, "Yes, we're in favor of devolution." To say to the British government, "Yes, we'll talk to you about possible models of devolution" and to say also to the British government, "Yes, we will agree that we will now jointly affirm that we want to see devolution happen" and that we in Dublin say, "We won't interpose ourselves between the parties to it, or between them and London, and we're prepared to define the parameters of Anglo-Irish relations in relation to the Northern Ireland scene in a post devolution situation."

And in the absence of an alternative to a unitary state, the government's policy, he says, is to "do nothing":

> The present impasse will continue until Fianna Fail comes down into the real world and sees that the unitary state by agreement is one goal that isn't going to happen, and they begin to act accordingly. That's a necessary condition for any progress but it probably isn't a sufficient condition. Some developments will be needed on the Unionist side, too.

And again, in contrast to Fianna Fail, Fine Gael does not believe that Article 1(c) suggests a change in policy for the British, from being pro-Union to being neutral on the Union. Dukes characterizes it as a shift in emphasis rather than a shift in position, a shift that makes explicit what is implicit in the Northern Ireland Constitution Act (1973). However, Dukes says, "If Fianna Fail could bring themselves to the belief that devolution is the inevitable next step – whether it's the final step or not, I don't know – then I think that we could reestablish a consensus."

Meanwhile, you have other obstacles to bringing the SDLP and the Unionists to the table. Says Dick Spring:

> The SDLP gives the impression of being more willing than the Unionists. But they don't have to do anything because they know the Unionists won't do anything. The Unionists tell us they will

not have anything to do with Dublin. The SDLP are telling [the Unionists] to talk to Dublin. The British are making remarks about devolved government. But nobody seems to know how to get the process in motion.

The Progressive Democrats, founded in 1985 – some time after Des O'Malley was expelled from Fianna Fail when he questioned Haughey's claim that the Forum Report called for a unitary Irish state and only a unitary state – are uncompromising devolutionists. "At the end of the day," Des O'Malley told the Progressive Democrats' annual conference in May 1989, two months before it would become part of the Fianna Fail Coalition, "the ultimate relationship that has to be resolved, if peace is ever to be attained, is between the two communities inside Northern Ireland."

"It [the relationship between the two communities within Northern Ireland] is basically more important than any of the other relationships," he says. "Moreover, [Unionists] are probably less likely to talk with Dublin until they have already had meaningful talks with the constitutional nationalists in the North." To encourage them, "[it should be] made clear that there is no great problem, basically, in the Anglo-Irish relationship, if the relationship on the ground within Northern Ireland could be sorted out." He would prefer that the SDLP give "a priority to the internal situation in the North" because "that's the hurdle that must be jumped over before the hurdle of the Unionist-Dublin relationship is sorted out." Indeed, he would go further: "Even if Taylor and Haughey were to have talks tomorrow morning," they wouldn't achieve very much "until things have normalized in the North." Normalization, in his view, means power sharing.

And to what degree can these views be reconciled with Fianna Fail's? "Up to the present," O'Malley says, "we've avoided the problem rather than reconciled it. Each of us knows where we stand. And we've avoided it because there hasn't been a crunch issue in the last four or five months while we've been in government." For the present there is a reprieve; their opposing views "haven't clashed because circumstances are such that, unfortunately, so little is happening in the positive sense, the problem hasn't really arisen."

On the question of devolution, O'Malley is emphatic. If he were Taoiseach, he would use Article 4 to push devolution with the British government. "The British and Irish governments," he says, "provided each of them had a determination to do so, could easily come to some agreement among themselves on the form that devolution should take." However, it would be essential for both of them "to involve the parties on the ground in the North." Can the Progressive Democrats push Haughey on devolution? "We are very much a minority party," says O'Malley, "and there's a limit to what we can do in regard to this, particularly since it's one that's very sensitive."

He agrees with Hume's interpretation of Article 1 as signalling a change in British policy from a position of being pro-Union to being politically neutral. "I think it's a significant thing," he says, "because for over half a century that wasn't their view. And I think that that is one of the most significant aspects of all of the Anglo-Irish Agreement."

But he is concerned that the Agreement isn't living up to its potential. "It should be dynamic and changing. And it isn't – that's the weakness of it, it has become somewhat bogged down. The spirit of it has died out ... There hasn't, for example, been a full-scale meeting between the Irish Taoiseach and the British Prime Minister since November 1985." And what could be done to get the dynamic back into the Agreement? "The approach they [the Irish government] should take would be devolution, [but] clearly you would [first] have to get the two leaders of the two communities in the North talking to one another. Both governments should press them a bit more. At the moment they're getting encouragement, but not pressure." In government, "what I would like to do," says O'Malley, "is to encourage gradual movement." In the meantime, "Our influence can be seen from another point of view, too – that we prevent certain things happening that might otherwise happen if we weren't there."

It is likely, therefore, that government policy will continue to be mainly reactive and ambivalent. There will be fewer mentions of "failed political entities", but fewer mentions, too, of devolution. In this area, the government will walk a fine line, remaining passive and excusing its inactivity on the grounds that the constitutional parties in the North must find their own way to the negotiating table and cannot be hurried by government arm-twisting.

Meanwhile, invitations to Unionists to talks with Dublin, especially within a European context, will continue to be issued. "It is," says Dukes, "a no-lose situation [for Haughey]. If they [Unionists] don't take up the offer, they will have turned down a very generous invitation on his part. If they did take up the offer, I think he'd dine out on it for a couple of years afterwards, because he would have [achieved] a historical break-through and had talks with the Unionists, even if they led to nothing."

When Brian Lenihan talks of the achievements of the Agreement he gives pride of place to its impact on Sinn Fein. In the South, he says, "Sinn Fein as a political party is practically gone. It doesn't command support and is unlikely to command support. The Anglo-Irish Agreement, if you like, has been the safety valve within which the South's constitutional opinion has found expression." In the North, there is a difference of degree: Sinn Fein and the IRA have been "marginalized" whereas in the South they have been "practically eliminated." "The number of people who believe in the Armalite and the ballot box has diminished. It's now down to a handful of very desperate people," says Lenihan. "And a handful can do it. Soft target options can be taken by a handful of desperate people. But it's down to that, and Sinn Fein's voting support, North and South, is dropping all the time."

Even if this is so – and many would dispute Lenihan's analysis – there is a broad-based consensus among the political parties in the South that the British government has no coherent strategy, no set of long-term goals that define the parameters of its policies in the North. Says Alan Dukes, "There are specific things they would like to get done. [But] other than that, there was no specific and identifiable corpus of Northern Ireland policy." Dick Spring agrees. "I don't think if you went over to 10 Downing Street," he says, "or to a Cabinet meeting and asked, 'What is the long-term policy of Her Majesty's government?', I don't think they could actually give you a two-page blueprint. I don't believe they have one, and I don't think they ever had one."

On the other hand, the opposition parties do not believe that the Irish government has a policy. "It's questionable," says Spring, "apart from the old aspiration of uniting Ireland"; and, for Dukes, "to the extent that they have one, it's a do-nothing policy."

"People," Spring says, "are afraid that if you talk about postponement, if you talk about suspension, that will be seen as a victory for the Unionists, and that, of course, would never do." Of course not. And this is, perhaps, the hidden, even unconscious agenda. At the moment, the greatest obstacle to talks may be a perceived historical half-truth: that the British always back down in the face of the threat of Unionist violence. Nationalists point to 1912 when officers of the British army stationed at the Curragh resigned their commissions rather than follow orders to march North to position themselves for an offensive drive on Ulster, should the Unionists make a unilateral declaration of independence. That once it was clear that the government could not rely on force to implement Home Rule for Ireland, partition of Ireland was inevitable. They point, too, to 1974 when the government refused to use the army to break the Ulster Workers' Council strike against the Sunningdale Agreement, thereby ensuring its collapse. These are half-truths because there is an implicit assumption that, had the British acted differently on both occasions, the outcomes would have been different, and that, consequently, the course of Irish history would have taken a different route. In short, if the Orange card had been called, it would have turned out to be a bluff; the Unionists would have capitulated. Hence Hume's insistence that "the British government must stand firm against any attempt by anybody to overthrow the democratic decisions of the British Parliament by force or threats of force."[96]

But the British government did not back down, and the Unionists, one is to assume, have learned their "lesson." However, the fear that lurks in the subterrane of the collective Nationalist consciousness is that they may not have, that a concession to any Unionist demand whatsoever has the potential to animate bad habits, re-ignite the old triumphalism – that accommodation will convince Unionists that intransigence always pays dividends. To the extent that Unionists are prisoners of that belief, Nationalists are prisoners, too, because ultimately it requires them to mimic the inaction of Unionists.

And thus the fatalism. "I don't see any scenario," says Spring. "We're in a stalemate [which we can't] break out of, which is obviously very depressing." "I don't see any immediate prospect of anything very constructive [emerging among the political parties in the North]," is Dukes' summary conclusion. For

Des O'Malley, "little is happening – the spirit of the Agreement has died." "The question of progress," says FitzGerald, "depends to a significant degree on two people: Molyneaux and Paisley. They, by simply staying there and doing nothing, can block progress, which suits them both for different reasons. They might remain for five years. One or the other or both of them may go, in which case some progress is possible." "You can't force people to join you at the conference table," says Lenihan. "What can you do, other than say, 'Come on' and put all the logic on the table for doing it? If people still want to say 'No', well, then, that's it. There is no other option [open] to us. I mean, we're in a ridiculous situation, candidly. It's not heartening, to put it mildly."

But one can, of course, look for a new framework: 1992. "We have a commonality of interests in the European context," says Spring, "and many Unionists in Northern Ireland are expressing the view that they would have been better represented by the Republic of Ireland Minister than they were by the British Minister in Brussels." The Single Market, abolishing national frontiers and establishing a market of 320 million consumers, will accelerate movement towards monetary and fiscal union – including a common European currency and a European central bank, and the harmonization of tax rates – that will make traditional concepts of sovereignty irrelevant, as nations voluntarily give up parts of their individual sovereignty in the common interests of the Community. Both parts of Ireland will share a commonality of interests in the emerging Europe, and as a single cohesive community develops, it will "further undermine the old arguments about its Border and [will challenge] those espousing both Nationalist and Unionist identities to reassess what they mean in real terms."[97]

Perhaps.

Britain

Northern Ireland is no longer an important item on Mrs. Thatcher's political agenda – not that it ever was much of one – and is likely to become even less of one as she makes her way through a difficult third term, beset with difficulties with her European colleagues and increasingly challenged within her own party. The myth of her invincibility has been shattered; bereft of her autocratic appurtenances, she is more vulnerable and more preoccupied with her own political problems.

She has, she feels, done her part and remains obdurate in the face of the Unionists' opposition to the Agreement, which deteriorated frequently into offensive personal attacks on her. Her relations with Mr. Haughey are coldly correct and formal. His actions during the Falklands war, which she regarded as an act of betrayal, are neither forgiven nor forgotten. One consequence is that there has been no formal Anglo-Irish summit meeting between the two Prime Ministers since Haughey became Taoiseach again in 1987. Their meetings, on the fringes of Economic Community summits, are brief and confined to exchanges relating whatever security problem of the day occupies center stage.

Throughout much of 1990, Peter Brooke, Secretary of State for Northern Ireland, tried to fill the political vacuum, to find some formula that would enable the constitutional parties, especially the Unionist parties, to participate in talks about future governance arrangements for Northern Ireland that would result in a new agreement, one to which all parties and both governments could give their support, and that would supersede the existing Anglo-Irish Agreement.[10]

Reviewing his first one hundred days in office, Brooke, told reporters that, "In terms of the late-20th century terrorist, organized as well as the Provisional IRA have become, it is difficult to envisage a military defeat of such a force because of the circum-stances in which they operate." If, however, the moment came "when they [the terrorists] wished to withdraw from their activities, then I think the government would need to be imagi-native in those circumstances as to how the process should be managed."[98] This remark elicited the usual storm of uproar in the Protestant community and was well received in the Catholic community, North and South. "Sinn Fein," Mr. Haughey said, "would be welcome to attend a constitutional conference if the IRA laid down its arms and abandoned violence."[99] Within weeks, Brooke had fallen back on the usual shibboleths: "Our aim is to defeat the terrorists and to bring these troubles to an end," he told the Derry Chamber of Commerce. "We shall not be deflected from our course, nor weary of our duty, nor shirk the cost."[100] And weeks later, he added other wrinkles: "The govern-ment recognizes that PIRA cannot be defeated by military means alone and that a concerted approach to security, political, and economic policies is necessary to ensure that terrorism is brought to an end",[101] and "The terrorist has made no progress. If any-thing, he has gone backwards because of the nature of Article One of the Agreement. With regard to Sinn Fein, there would be no question of entering into dialogue as long as that party continues to support the use of force to achieve political objec-tives."[102]

Peter Brooke is the second Secretary of State to administer Northern Ireland since the signing of the Agreement. In five months on the job, he has learned the pitfalls of language and the potential firestorm that can overwhelm the most casual observa-tions. He is diplomatically correct, appropriately careful.

On the question of British neutrality: The British government, he says, is not politically neutral on Northern Ireland. "The Brit-ish government in signing the Treaty," he says, "is committing itself that if there were the desire to negotiate the status of [Northern Ireland] by constitutional means, that [it] would participate in that process." In his view, this "is not markedly different than the position of the British government going the whole way back to 1920"; in that sense, therefore, "it does not represent a new statement." Moreover, "the party that sustains the present government remains the Conservative and Unionist Party, and the Prime Minister, as the leader of that party, has made clear that her views are supportive of the Union." However, "the present government ... is sustained by a party which does have particular views [regarding the Union]"; Hume would have "a fairly large task if he was actually seeking to move the party to change this position." That position, however, he is at pains to point out, would not necessarily be the position "of a government of a different political hue."

On the question of the Union itself: The Conservative Party "would wish very much to see Northern Ireland remain part of the Union." Accordingly, the conclusion Hume draws from his observation that the British were neutral, that it was now up to Nationalists to get Britain to join the ranks of the persuaders, "would be a false analysis if it was thought that the British government was part of the process of seeking to exercise that element of persuasion." He "[is] not part of the process, nor is the government part of the process of urging Unionists to go." Inducing consent is "not part of [his] strategy and not the government's strategy."

And as to Hume's statement that he was looking for "an agreement that would transcend in importance any agreement ever made", neither Brooke nor the NIO has asked Hume what he means by this. But if it indicates Hume's interest in "some kind of definitive settlement between the Unionist people and the rest of the people of the island," Brooke says that, "given my preference for negotiation in a lowish voice and with a lowish profile, with a concentration on the workable, then I don't actually think that ambitions, which seem to me to be too large for our present ability, do advance matters."

However, if Brooke is politely critical with elements of the SDLP perspectives regarding the way forward and the assumptions underpinning the broader SDLP/Fianna Fail strategy, he is no less politely critical of the Unionists' perspectives and strategies. He would take issue with the Unionist contention that the Agreement is a failure. He does not accept Unionist contentions that Anglo-Irish relations are worse, that the Agreement has been ineffective, that its ineffectiveness is due in large measure to the effectiveness of the Unionist campaign against it, and that the way forward is for the two governments to admit their failure and call the parties together to come up with a workable arrangement. Unionists, he says, "have the problem of having elevated a tactic in the first instance into a principle." As a result, "not only have [they] some difficulty in moving from the ground they have chosen to take up, but they also have an interest in observations about the Agreement and attribution of their actions to the consequences and to what has happened, which we might not find ourselves mutually in agreement on." He would, therefore, disagree with their analysis.

The position Unionists have that the Union has been weakened, that the British can't wait until consent for a united Ireland emerges so that they can unload Northern Ireland into an all-Ireland state, is, he insists, "absolutely not the case." But "the exercise of demonstrating that that is not the case, with the Anglo-Irish Agreement in being, is a test [for the] government." He admires the Unionists "for their staunchness in a particular cause." They would, he believes, "think less of me and less of the government if the government were making concessions on its commitment to the Anglo-Irish Agreement, whether or not it responds to the campaign that they wage." If the government, he argues, "is inconstant in the context of the Agreement, one's words in the context of the Union would themselves be less persuasive." In other words, the tenaciousness of the government commitment to the Agreement, despite Unionists pressures on it, is a barometer of its tenaciousness on the Union. Just as it would stand up to Unionists on the Agreement, it would stand up to Nationalists on the Union. Nevertheless, he does allow "that convincing the Unionists that the Union is, if anything, stronger as a result of the Agreement, because of the endorsement by the Irish government of the principle of majority consent in Article One, is a task which embraces the whole of government and the whole of the majority community." Moreover, he is "sufficiently a working politician to recognize that if you actually wish to move forward from where we now are, you're going to have to take into account the position that the Unionists hold."

The Agreement works: "[It] had a number of purposes," he says, "and taken all in all, the Agreement has conferred more benefits than otherwise ... On pragmatic grounds, the Agreement works effectively in terms of working out differences between ourselves and the government of the Republic." Devolution still remains elusive, but the prospects for it are "if anything better than they were at the time I assumed office." "We are moving forward," he says, "[and while we're not] moving forward fast, we are moving forward rather than backwards ... I do believe that the Agreement can be operated sensitively, in the interests of bringing about talks between the political parties and giving them the best possible chance of success."

Government policy is founded on the principle of consent. In other words, says Brooke, "the status of Northern Ireland should be determined by the wishes of a majority of the people living there." As long as it is the wish of the majority to remain part of the United Kingdom "the government will support and uphold that wish." The reality is that "for the foreseeable future Northern Ireland will not cease to be part of the United Kingdom." The principle of majority consent "is enshrined in the Northern Ireland Act (1973) and was reaffirmed by both governments in Article One of the Anglo-Irish Agreement."

On Mr. Brooke's part there are no ambiguities on the question of consent. But the fact is that despite the plethora of declarations, communiques, statements, and expositions, the issue of consent continues to bedevil the Northern Ireland question and, instead of encouraging a gradual cross-community consensus developing in the North on constitutional matters, Article One contributes to divisiveness. Unionists are assured time and again that their status will not be changed without the consent of a majority, and insofar as that consent isn't there, that their status will remain unchanged. Nationalists are told that if they can get the numbers to support a united Ireland, one will follow. Nationalists want the British to send a signal to the Unionist community that closer links with the South are in the Unionists' best interest. Nationalists believe that once they can persuade Britain to join the ranks of the persuaders, Unionist consent to a united Ireland will follow – not immediately or enthusiastically, perhaps, but nevertheless inevitably, when the realization that they have no other viable options finally sinks in.

In other words, for Nationalists, the Agreement is a stage in a process leading ultimately at some unspecified time to a predetermined outcome. "… [U]ntil such time as something better or more acceptable can be negotiated and agreed to take its place," says Haughey, "the present Agreement will stand."[103] "Better" or "more acceptable" mean, of course, something closer to a united Ireland. Nationalists, therefore, are encouraged, if only inadvertently, to make Northern Ireland unworkable, to frustrate attempts to find internal solutions, to drive home to both the British and the Unionists that a Northern Ireland within a United Kingdom context is a failed political entity, incapable of being remoulded, thus begging the question: If not in a United Kingdom context, then in what sort of a context?

Accordingly, both traditions are encouraged to pursue their antipodean aspirations: Nationalists, to "persuade" what they see as a "neutral" Britain – a characterization the British government has not hitherto bothered to either deny or clarify – to put her shoulder behind the goal of an all-Ireland state; Unionists, to hang together so that the solidarity of their numbers precludes such a possibility.

The unquenchable Nationalist conviction is that, in the long run, Britain will do whatever suits her own interests. "Let me remind you [the media]," Brooke said during his interview marking his first one hundred days in office, "of the move towards independence in Cyprus, and the British Minister stood up in the House of Commons and used the word 'Never' in a way in which, in two days, there had been a retreat from that word."[104] Almost immediately Brooke would regret the analogy of Northern Ireland to Cyprus; for Nationalists, however, it was the word 'Never' that lingered.

Nationalists remember British 'Nevers', remember the innumerable times the British have used the word in distant places over the years; they know that 'Never' is part of a public moral vocabulary and that when it is convenient, the British always find a way to subordinate their moral vocabulary to the politics of pragmatism, a politics they practice with consummate skill. Nationalist leaders who talk in terms of change take pains to eschew the issue of constitutional status altogether. For the most part, their listeners know what they're saying, especially when it's left unsaid. When John Hume and Charles Haughey talk about "agreements that will transcend other agreements" and new governance structures that will enable the two traditions to "share the island of Ireland" without specifically making it clear that such arrangements would take place within existing constitutional frameworks, Unionists have every right to believe that "talks" mean acquiescence to some undefined change that will bring a united Ireland closer. For Nationalists, talks – even talks without preconditions – are political statements of intent; the only matter to be settled is the form the outcome will take, rather than the nature of the outcome itself.

Under the umbrella of the principle of consent there are, says Brooke, three elements to British policy. They are: "A security policy, whose purpose is to see the ending of terrorism; a policy for political development, which intends to secure the transfer of authority and power to local politicians; and a social and economic policy to improve the condition of the people throughout the province – to get rid of barriers and to secure through a variety of means a basis for fairness across the whole community." The complications, he says, arise from trying to manage these three strands of policy simultaneously. The government recognizes "that you must secure the ending of terrorism by drawing on a security policy which seeks to deny the terrorists freedom of movement and action." But that policy "[has to be] reinforced by the policy relating to political development and social and economic development." In this regard, the politicians of Northern Ireland have not been playing their part; they can, he says, "make a larger contribution towards ending terrorism by participating in the process."

Because of the political deadlock, the Conference – which met on thirty occasions between 1985 and the end of 1989 – has become, to an inappropriate degree, a forum for discussion of security measures or for ironing out differences in security-related matters. It has largely failed to address political matters, especially those relating to devolution. No proposals regarding devolution have been put before it. Moreover, it took the government almost two years to publicly respond to the devolution proposals Molyneaux and Paisley submitted to the NIO in January 1988, and to "welcome the continuing commitment of the Unionist leadership to seek progress from that starting point".[105] He is, Brooke says, "ready to facilitate agreement on the arrangements for interparty talks, and to discuss the steps the government might take to help." And while much needs to be done, there is, in his judgment, "enough common ground to make worthwhile the start of talks soon on new arrangements for exercising political power in Northern Ireland."[106]

Meanwhile, the government applies itself elsewhere: to the economic revitalization of Belfast; to economic and social assistance programs specifically targeted at ghetto areas, especially in Republican strongholds; to the elimination of employment discrimination through the Fair Employment (Northern Ireland) Act (1989), which sets out the statutory requirements for hiring Catholics and Protestants, procedures for eliminating unfair hiring practices and for encouraging fair ones, and timetables and monitoring measures to ensure compliance; to the promotion of integrated education through the Education Reform (Northern Ireland) Order (1989) which will provide special assistance for integrated schools and begin to harmonize school curricula.

And in other areas the government has made more controversial moves: modifying a defendant's right to remain silent during questioning and trial to allow courts to draw whatever inference they may deem proper from the fact that an accused person remains silent; prohibiting, except at election time, access to radio and television by "extremist organizations" (including Sinn Fein and the UDA); making additions to the Public Order Act (1986) to impose restrictions, including prohibitions, on public processions, marches, and open-air meetings. However, preoccupation with the security situation – the unrelenting drive to contain the IRA – remains on the front burner and continues, as in the past, to set the political agenda rather than vice-versa.

But it is, perhaps, in matters relating to security policies that the soft underbelly of the Agreement is most exposed. At the heart of the alienation of the minority community is the security issue. The security forces are seen to be oppressive, harassing, and abusive. The UDR and RUC are overwhelmingly Protestant, which virtually puts one community in the position of policing the other. The judicial system is seen as discriminatory and unjust. The Diplock Courts, with the one judge-no jury system, have few adherents. The powers of arrest in the Emergency Provisions Act are invariably used against Catholics. However, to the Protestant community, security means an entirely different thing. Members of the UDR and RUC – in the frontline of the battle against terrorists, servants of the state and the upholders of the law – are primary targets of the IRA. When they are shot, the Protestant community sees the killings as the murder of Protestants because their positions make them identifiably Protestant. When the issue of security comes up, therefore, not only is there a difference in perception with regard to what the problem is, there are even greater differences in the two communities in the levels of intensity with which these perceptions are held. There is no way in the short run – and, perhaps, not even in the long run – for these two entirely different perceptions of the security problem to be reconciled so as to develop a policing system acceptable to the two communities in Northern Ireland. If anything, the situation has probably become worse in recent times when evidence of collusion between Loyalist paramilitary groups and members of the RUC and the UDR – who were supplying them with photographic montages of suspected members of the IRA – came to light. Few Catholics were surprised. For most, it reinforced what their history would have taught them. "I don't think you're going to see a circumstance in the foreseeable future," says Seamus Mallon, "where the RUC will be accepted in a meaningful way in the mainstream Catholic areas." But without that acceptance, the SDLP's participation in a devolved government becomes more problematic.

The Labour Party, according to the party manifesto on Northern Ireland, continues "to have fundamental differences with the present British government" over Article 1(c). "We do not believe," it says, "that it is responsible or adequate to await passively the dawning of consent, as the Government does. The Labour Party, by contrast, is committed to working actively to build that consent."[107]

Insofar as the Labour Party has a clearly defined objective that is pro-Irish unity, it has a more coherent policy than the Conservative Party, which has not so much as policy as a series of policies. Moreover, it is unlikely that Brooke's exposition of government policy would change many minds from the view that the government has no policy, in part because the espoused policy lacks a clear sense of direction; in part because its three elements often operate at cross-purposes, especially when the pursuit of security-related objectives puts obstacles in the way of achieving political objectives; and in part because the political will to aggressively push a devolution agenda is absent. "Mrs. Thatcher," John Alderdice observes, "tends to say 'This is my policy and I'm going to force it through, whether you like it or not.' On the question of devolution for Northern Ireland, which is the stated policy, she hasn't done that."

The government should declare itself unequivocally on the neutrality question, and indicate whether it believes that the Unionists' future would be better assured and their interests better accommodated within some all-Ireland framework. If it does, it should give Unionists the opportunity to assess their position and evaluate their alternatives. If, however, the government and the party are pro-Union, that should be made unambiguously clear so that Nationalists, who are building a strategy on the assumption that Britain is neutral, can stop fooling themselves, or at least bide their time until the Labour Party comes to power.

But it is naive to believe that a Labour Party government would be any more successful than a Conservative one in forging some consensus between the two communities. The Labour Party talks of "the broad support of the people of Northern Ireland" as being a precondition for unity. But majority support is not necessarily broad support, and majoritarianism, it has been argued, is not a useful concept in the context of Northern Ireland. Can you design a policy to achieve something that is not foreseeable? And what secret prescriptions does Labour have that would "start changing the minds and hearts of the Northern Loyalist community to [the Agreement]" when its pro-unity position stands in the way of achieving the trust of the Unionist community (which will read a "pro-unity" intention into every government action), when its hostile non-cooperation in every area of the political economy will simply further divide the two divided communities?

And what if the inequities Catholics face in employment and the abuse of their rights in the administration of justice and the actions of the security forces are dealt with to their satisfaction?

What if all the social and economic deprivation they have been subjected to is alleviated to their satisfaction? And what if the Irish government continues to have a role as a guarantor of their rights and constitutional Nationalists legislate on their behalf in a Northern Ireland Assembly? Would they be satisfied with that or would they want something more? Would they still want unity?

But the numbers aren't there for unity – and may never be there. That is a reality Nationalists cannot face: that the aspiration will remain just that, an aspiration, capable of being articulated, but incapable, perhaps, of being achieved. Ironically, Unionists won't face it, either; for all their trust in their numbers, their faith is too weak. And how can they ever trust the Catholic community – or the South or the British, for that matter – when they live in permanent fear that, in the end, they will be sold out by their own?

Toward New Frameworks

At its annual conference in October 1989, the Conservative Party voted to support the affiliation of the North Down association. Weeks later, the National Union of Conservative Associations gave its imprimatur when it admitted three other associations as well, thus ensuring that in the future the Conservative Party would contest elections in the North.

The reaction in Nationalist Ireland was revealing. The *Irish News*, the daily newspaper of the broad Catholic middle in the North, came out against the decision. "In Ireland as a whole," it said in an editorial, "the move will be received as a retrograde step for a party such as the Conservatives to become entangled in Northern Ireland elections, particularly when the British government has been working towards a more neutral stand through the workings of the Anglo-Irish Agreement."[108]

Des O'Malley called the Conservative Party's action "negative and somewhat insensitive" and "contrary to the recognition of the Nationalist aspiration which is contained in the Anglo-Irish Agreement."[109] The SDLP party whip Eddie McGrady argued that government Ministers could no longer act as "honest brokers," that with Tory representation on the ground the Conservative government "could not be seen to be an impartial broker" in a negotiating situation. Seamus Mallon said that "it tells [Nationalists] something about the Tory political mind about Northern Ireland", that "the strand towards integration within the Tory party [was] strong", that its decision to organize was, therefore, "an indication towards integration".[110] Even the *Irish Times* weighed in with the opinion that "the message to the North would be integrationist not devolutionist", an interpretation which would cast "doubt on the durability" of the Anglo-Irish Agreement.[111] In short, a broad cross-section of Nationalist opinion believes that it is somehow contrary to the intention of the Agreement that Unionists should actually have the opportunity to vote for the party which governs them.

Conservative Party organization in the North suggests closer links between Britain and Northern Ireland;[11] this, too, in the eyes of Nationalists appears to be sleight-of-hand, contrary to the spirit of the Agreement – the spirit, in their view, being the suggestion of a concerted campaign to persuade Britain to help persuade Unionists that their future lies in working out a new relationship with the South. The corollary here is that while Nationalists demand that their rights and aspirations be accorded due respect and a place in the process, there is a peculiar reluctance to accept that Unionists should have equally unfettered rights. If the Nationalist task is to persuade Britain "to join the ranks of the persuaders", to try and move it from being "neutral" to being "pro-Irish unity", surely, using the same logic, Unionists have the right to persuade Britain to protect the Union, to try and move it from being "neutral" to being more aggressively "pro-Union." And when Nationalists clearly state their aspirations for a united Ireland and form coalitions, create processes, and mobilize international pressure to give impetus to their aspirations, surely Unionists are right to regard new governance arrangements which Nationalists propose as being Trojan horses. "I would like to see the Irish Republic recognize that, if we as Northern Unionists have to recognize the aspirations of the Nationalists' views, then the Nationalist people in the Republic have got to recognize the aspirations of the Unionists," says Martin Smyth. To Nationalists, that would appear to be somehow counterintuitive.

Implicit in Nationalists' apprehension about mainland British party participation in the politics of Northern Ireland is the belief that these parties have no business being there, that it makes no difference whether the people of Northern Ireland have the opportunity to vote for the parties which govern their country – precisely because Nationalists do not believe that Northern Ireland in a United Kingdom context is part of *their* country and do not think in terms of Unionists having a right to think of it as being part of theirs. Anything, therefore, that would give a more concrete expression to the North being a part of a nation called the United Kingdom of Great Britain and Northern Ireland must be reactively opposed – it interferes with the imagining of the conflict. Partition, in the end, is psychological rather than physical.

There would also appear to be a certain double standard to the Nationalists' perspective. They take it for granted that political parties in the South, whether in government or out of government, should act as surrogates on their behalf. Indeed, the Irish government, under the auspices of the Intergovernmental Conference, is unabashedly non-neutral – and the process is designed to ensure that that "non-neutral" voice will be heard and listened to. Unionists, however, have no surrogate. It would be difficult to argue that the British government – which deliberately kept Unionists uninformed during the discussions leading to the Anglo-Irish Agreement – is an advocate for Unionist interests or that Unionists have a forum they might use to promote their interests. The Conservative Party would, of course, provide such a forum by integrating a section of Unionist opinion into the mainstream of British policies. But again, anything that would appear to make Northern Ireland a more integral part of the U.K. is an anathema to Nationalists. Their policies, after all, are aimed at exploiting and exaggerating differences between the two, in part because it underscores the separateness of the North, and in part because it allows a more facile comparison of interests between the North and the South.

However, once it is conceded that Unionists have as much a right to their aspirations, and to doing their utmost to persuade Britain that it is in her interest to strengthen the Union, as Nationalists have to their aspirations, and to doing their utmost (constitutionally) to persuade Britain that it is in her interest to encourage Irish unity, the Agreement becomes an instrument of polarization. A "neutral" Britain becomes a potential consort to be wooed, to be unrelentingly importuned by both traditions to their points of view – each tradition diligently dissecting every action of the other for its impact on British opinion, the action of one inviting a countervailing action of the other, each adding more suspicion and distrust to the centuries of suspicion and mistrust, each attempting to undercut the other at every opportunity. It encourages competition between the traditions rather than cooperation. It becomes, in fact, the guarantor of sectarian solidarity.

Which brings up the ignored centerpiece of the conflict – ignored not in the sense of its having gone unstated but in the sense of there being an unwillingness to confront the consequences that follow from it. Jim Prior addressed it bluntly during the Commons debate on the New Ireland Forum Report and Peter Brooke reiterates it today: "There is one overriding and abiding reality," Prior told the House, "and that is that consent is simply not forthcoming for any formulation that denies the Unionists their rights not only to belong to the United Kingdom but to be apart from the Republic."[112] Nationalists acknowledge the Unionist right to withhold consent only in the most perfunctory way – not because they believe out of conviction that Unionists have an inherent right to withhold consent, but in the practical sense that you can't force a million people in an island of five million to do what they patently do not want to do. The reality of the situation is acknowledged – but not the legitimacy of it.

The Fianna Fail-PD government and the SDLP simply ignore the issues raised by the obvious absence of consent among Unionists for any form of association with the South, and they fail to address what ought to be done in the here and now, since consent will not be forthcoming in the foreseeable future – if ever. Nationalists simply side-step the issue: Their task is to "convince" Unionists; and to this end, they use each new process as a stepping stone to another process, each making the concept of consent itself more amorphous, each calling for "new relationships", each ambiguously coded, each implicitly suggesting that Unionists' refusal to come to their senses – that is, follow the Nationalists' course of action – makes them somehow culpable for the violence to which their community is exposed. When

Hume says that Unionists must settle the relationships now or be a party to Northern Ireland becoming "a very ugly backwater" the insinuation is clear. Unless matters are settled now, the IRA's armed campaign will continue to stay its wretched course, and constitutional Nationalists will wash their hands of responsibility for whatever repercussions that might have in the Protestant community.

This thoughtless conviction among Nationalists that a united Ireland will ineluctably rise, Phoenix-like, out of the detritus of the sectarian miasma enveloping the North, inhibits dialogue, reinforces Protestant sectarian solidarity (since nothing can be taken at face value), and compels Unionists to look only for the deceit that must inform, in their view, every Catholic gesture of accommodation. And thus Hume's appeals to Unionists to embark on a process leading to an "agreement that would transcend in importance any agreement ever made" or to decide on arrangements to "share the island" to their (Catholic and Protestant) "mutual satisfaction", and his stress on "the equality of the two traditions", are grist for the mill of Unionist distrust. They hear him differently, and when they translate his language into theirs, they see coercion, not accommodation, as the message Hume delivers.

Seeking to convince Unionists of the benefits of a new relationship with the rest of Ireland is an acceptable strategy within reason, but when the effort to elicit that consent becomes an end in itself – the tactic elevated to the level of principle – when the language of persuasion lacks a syntax for consensus, at some point the relentless pursuit of the mathematics of consent becomes counterproductive and the attempt to persuade becomes an act of harassment. The act of seeking consent changes the context in which it is perceived; the distinction between it being freely given or induced by an attrition of alternatives becomes artificial. It changes the dimension of the problem it is supposed to address and once again reinforces Unionist perceptions that all Nationalist actions serve one purpose only: to bring about a united Ireland. In the course of a statement he released on 31 October 1989 Alan Dukes said that "... the prospect of a unitary state being achieved by agreement in one step is utterly unreal", that "reality dictates practical but smaller steps", that "the first step towards peace is for the people of Northern Ireland to govern their own lives", that "that is what devolution means."[113] "Even putting it in those terms," says Alderdice, "leads Unionists to say 'So he is saying a devolved government is a stepping stone to a united Ireland' ... Everything that has happened to Unionists in the last twenty years suggests to [them] that they're going to be forced against their will into something or other." The Agreement simply vindicated their paranoia. As a result, even token gestures that would recognize common interests are impossible because they might be interpreted as acquiescence to the Nationalist agenda. When every action might become an allegorical statement of betrayal, action is simply eschewed.

A further, not unrelated, problem is that language in whatever form – whether spoken words, treaties, or statutes – has little literal meaning for either tradition. Everything is used to reinforce prior perceptions. "People tend to interpret things," says Alderdice, "to suit their own mythology." An impartial observer, for example, would acknowledge that the Agreement guarantees the Unionists' place in the United Kingdom, as long as that is the will of the majority of the people there, yet that is the one thing Unionists ignore. They perceive an imagined relationship between the North and South rather than an actual relationship between the North and Britain. Similarly, an impartial observer would acknowledge that the Agreement pointedly recognizes the absence of consent in the North for a change in status, yet that is the one thing Nationalists ignore. They perceive an imagined situation in which consent is achieved; the promise of what would happen if consent were to emerge displaces the actual relationship between the North and South. For constitutionalists on both sides, the ingrained values of their symbolic reference points distort the language of political discourse, making serious dialogue difficult because there is not a language of dialogue to which they both subscribe.

But there is, at least, some common ground: All parties to the conflict believe negotiations should be going on. But who should attend those negotiations, the areas of discussion they should involve, how the process itself should unfold, and under whose auspices they should be held are questions over which there are widespread differences. Moreover, both Unionists and Nationalists have widely differing perceptions regarding their understanding of the last four years and the respective reasons why they and their opponents would want to come to the table. Furthermore, there is a fundamental and perhaps insoluble difference regarding the purpose of talks themselves: whether Nationalists would see them as just one more step in a continually unfolding process that would ultimately lead to a united Ireland or as an attempt to arrive at a permanent solution that would, perhaps, fall short of a united Ireland; and whether Unionists would see them as a final settlement that would establish once and for all that a united Ireland was out of the question, or as one more step in a process that would leave the issue of unity on the sidelines for the time being. Hume's suggestion that two referenda be held on the same day in both parts of Ireland would appear to indicate that he is thinking in terms of a final settlement; but for the moment, the SDLP, as in much else, are mute on the question.

The following provides a context for understanding what

must be taken into consideration if a successful dialogue is to ensue:

● Every party acknowledges that there are three interrelated problems. However, there is significant disagreement as to the order of importance of those relationships. While the SDLP and Fianna Fail would argue that the Unionist versus the rest-of-Ireland relationship is the core relationship that must be resolved and the pivot for more wide-ranging discussions, the Unionist parties, the Alliance Party, the Workers' Party, Fine Gael, Labour, the Progressive Democrats, and the British government believe that the relationship between the two communities within Northern Ireland must be addressed before the North-South relationship can be resolved. This does not mean that the parties, other than the Unionist parties, would not welcome Dublin-Unionist talks; they simply regard undue emphasis on them as being distracting and an avoidance of the real issues at hand.

● The Unionist parties totally distrust Hume's overtures for talks with Dublin and Haughey's invitations to come visit him. They see the former as an excuse on Hume's part for not engaging in talks with Unionists and thus being in a position to shift responsibility for the impasse onto Unionist shoulders – or as a ruse to legitimate talks in a North-South context, making it appear that Unionists concede the South's legitimate interests in the North. They see the latter as the politics of expedience, the grand gesture on Haughey's part that faintly conceals a "'Come into my parlor,' said the spider to the fly" intention. In reality, Unionist talks with Dublin are, given their avowed disposition, probably a long way off; if they take place at all, they will take place only after talks among the parties in the North are well under way. To focus on them to the exclusion of interparty talks in the North is to guarantee a continuing impasse and under-mine the intent of the Anglo-Irish Agreement. However, even if interparty talks in the North do occur, it does not appear that the SDLP would use the occasion to explore devolution options but, to quote Seamus Mallon, to "promote and explain [its] analysis of the situation, and to persuade them [Unionists] of the need for proper types of negotiations", i.e., to convince Unionists of the need for them to talk with Dublin.

● The SDLP is not interested in devolution *per se*. Indeed, devolution is a word that it prefers to eschew because of the pejorative connotation it has of power being something either "bestowed" or "withheld" by the British government. Nor is it clear whether it would look for devolution within the frame-work of the Northern Ireland Constitution Act (1973) or even in the context of the Anglo-Irish Agreement itself. At the very least, party whip Eddie McGrady believes "some tinkering" with the 1973 Act will be necessary. However, the SDLP has no coherent policy position, other than the aspiration to unity with consent (which is the iteration of an ideal rather than a statement of policy) and the commitment to a series of processes (mostly involving other parties) that are intended to create political configurations (mostly involving other parties) that alter the conditions which define the parameters of consent.

● Many Unionist leaders in both the OUP and the DUP – but especially the DUP – believe that a new agreement should involve "a redefined" relationship between Northern Ireland and the rest of the U.K. This redefinition would involve a loosening of the link between the two. To this extent, many Unionist leaders also contemplate modifications to the 1973 Act.

● There is no common agreement in the Unionist commu-nity on what form devolution should take or the nature of the mandate it should have. Within the Official Unionist Party, there are as many strands of opinion as there are party leaders. The party is significantly divided between the two major wings – that is, devolutionists of one brand or another and integrationists – making the development of a comprehensive policy position unlikely. While Official Unionists say they are ready to talk, the evidence at the moment suggests that they would run into difficulties once interparty talks moved into substantive areas. The "Do Nothing" posture the party has adopted since the signing of the Agreement works to the advantage of the integrationists. There is a growing belief that the inaction on the local political level in the last four years had the unintended effect of incubating integration – something that was the byproduct of bureaucratic exigency rather than political design. While Hume and Haughey may be content to outwait the Unionists, secure in the potential of the Agreement as it takes greater institutional hold each year, many of their colleagues – and many on the other side of the political divide – believe that further integration of Northern Ireland into the U.K. will continue to proceed on an arbitrary, ad hoc basis. The net result may be a Northern Ireland in which the Union has grown unwittingly stronger, and also one in which the Irish government speaks increasingly for Catholic Nationalists – a condominium situation with overtones of joint authority that becomes the solution of last resort instead of any party's preferred solution.

● Both the SDLP and the DUP would look for a maximum devolution of legislative powers for a Northern Ireland that would find its place somewhere between independence and autonomy. Whether that autonomy would lie within a U.K. or all-Ireland framework will not only be the point of divergence but one of immutable difference.

● For the DUP, talks are likely to be used to evaluate the constitutional options open to it. The insinuation, from both Robinson and Paisley, is that the DUP would seek some form of negotiated independence if it found that the price of maintaining the Union was too high in regard to the relationship with the South to which it would be forced to agree.

● With few exceptions, major elements of constitutional nationalism – including the SDLP, Fianna Fail, and the Progressive Democrats – contend that under Article 1(c) of the Agreement, the British have committed themselves to being "neutral" on Northern Ireland; i.e., that the government is no longer pro-Union in its outlook. *This shared and apparently mistaken assumption, at least in regard to the present British government, is the basis of the SDLP's and the Irish government's policy orientation.* With the undue emphasis, to quote Mr. Haughey, it puts on "persuading our Unionist countrymen that their future lies with us in a partnership of equals" and in "convincing the British government that the future of Ireland could and should be left to all the Irish people to decide for themselves",[114] it impedes reconciliation among the parties in Northern Ireland and between the two parts of Ireland.

To the extent that the assumption is false – both because of the British government's own position on the Union and the Conservative Party's expressed commitment to the Union, reflected in its decision to organize Conservative associations in the North and to contest elections there – the British government should declare itself forcefully on the issue. If it does not – and its silence encourages the supposition that it is neutral – it, too, becomes a catalyst for polarization.

● Despite the New Ireland Forum and the Anglo-Irish Agreement, there continues to be no consensus in the South regarding the way forward in the North. In particular, there are sharp and clear-cut differences between Fianna Fail's opposition to devolution and holding out for an all-party constitutional conference and the commitment of the other parties – Fine Gael, the Progressive Democrats, the Workers' Party, and Labour – to the belief that "all roads forward pass through devolution."[115] In the South, Northern Ireland remains on the back burner, a non-issue for most. It is likely to remain there because of the continuing high level of support for the Anglo-Irish Agreement.[116] Because Fianna Fail and Progressive Democrats have antithetical positions on devolution, their coalition in government narrows the options for discussion and, hence, for action, if the coalition is not to come under severe stress. Furthermore, the opposition parties in the South who favor devolution are unwilling to press their case as long as John Hume does not give it his imprimatur. Unionists close ranks despite differences. So, too, do Southern Nationalists behind Hume; to be out of sync with him is to undercut him; to criticize or question his judgment is to invite disparagement of one's motives; to advocate an alternative position is to stand accused of making constitutional nationalism in the North more vulnerable to either Sinn Fein propaganda or Unionist attack.

But without a consensus in the South, the problem in the North cannot be resolved. This absence of consensus would further undermine Hume's proposals for a double referendum. Given the swift demise of FitzGerald's Constitutional Crusade when attitudes toward it became a litmus test of domestic political allegiance, and given that consensus with regard to the New Ireland Forum Report took less time to evaporate than for the ink of its signatories to dry, a referendum on wider, more far-reaching proposals involving constitutional change seems dubious at best, factious at worst.

More importantly, the proposal as envisaged by Hume could never be endorsed by the Unionists, since it would permit a situation in which a governance package might be passed in the North but rejected in the South. Since Hume's proposal requires that the package must be passed by majorities in both jurisdictions, Unionists interpret it as an arrangement that would give the South a veto over how the North should be governed, which is, of course, unacceptable to them. But the principle of a dual referendum has merits. It implies a consensual approach to governance arrangements rather than a one-shot, up or down vote. If nothing else, it is an ideal gauge, encouraging modification that would make it viable.

● Taking literally the SDLP's declarations that it is prepared to negotiate an agreement that "will transcend in importance any agreement ever made" and its less-than- enthusiastic support for the devolution called for by the Agreement, it better suits the SDLP agenda to structure talks outside rather than within the framework of the Agreement. The Agreement calls specifically for interparty talks, under the stewardship of the Secretary of State, to explore devolution – a process that is not in harmony with the SDLP's contention that the Dublin-Unionist relationship is the axis on which all other relationships revolve. Unionists do not understand how inconsequential the Conference might become if acceptable cross-community governance arrangements were to emerge.

● There are important, indeed irreconcilable, differences in the perceptions of the two communities regarding the efficacy of the Agreement. Nationalist leaders (and the British government) believe that it has worked sufficiently well – especially in the areas of Anglo-Irish relations and the intangible but significantly important voice Northern Nationalists feel they now have in the process – to continue to voice their support for it. Nationalists also believe that the Unionist bluff has been called and found wanting, that Unionist opposition to the Agreement has petered out, that Unionists are undergoing a crisis of identity that will finally resolve itself on the side of a closer association with the rest of Ireland (especially when the implementation of the Single European Act takes effect in 1992, making the Border irrelevant – at least in a political/geographic sense – and the common interests of the island as a unit, as the peripheral region in the Community, become more obvious, compelling joint action on many fronts to protect mutual concerns.) In short, they believe that once Unionists are faced down, their threat to fight simply will evaporate, that the Unionist bark is worse than the Unionist bite, that the Unionist will to resist is by and large broken, and that it is only a matter of time before Unionists swallow their pride and come to their senses. Accordingly, any action, no matter how minuscule, that would make a concession, no matter how small, to Unionists regarding a suspension or dilution of the Agreement's workings is out of the question – so ingrained in the Nationalist psyche is the myth of the power of the Protestant veto. On this Hume is adamant: Anything that would allow Unionists even to whisper that they had successfully brought the Agreement to a halt, no matter how temporarily, that their years of protest had yielded a dividend, no matter how paltry, isn't on. They have to accept the fact that on this occasion, at least, they have lost. They must be taught a lesson, and the lesson is an integral part of the learning curve. "I will not agree to the suspension [of the workings of the Agreement] because that is the restoration of the [Protestant] veto," says Hume. "It would be a very serious mistake. If the British government backs down, you will never solve the Irish problem because you would have for the third time this century that happening."[117]

● Unionist perceptions of events are almost diametrically the opposite. But they are also more complicated. The low incidence of violence that accompanied the protest to the Agreement was, they believe, due entirely to their responsible leadership and the effectiveness of their efforts at the grassroots level to keep the protest under control. They feel their success in controlling the violence was not appreciated, and that the relative absence of violence was used against them in a manner that impugned their campaign.

They believe the Agreement has been an unmitigated disaster, that it has failed to deliver on any of the four objectives it was intended to achieve, that it has worsened Anglo-Irish relations. They further believe that the failure of the Agreement can be attributed, in substantial part, to their principled opposition to it, to the inherent contradictions in the Agreement itself, and to how the its framers paid little attention to the fact that for the Agreement to work, it had to have the cooperation of Unionists, without which the devolution it envisaged would remain a pipe dream – that while both governments anticipated Unionist opposition, they did not anticipate intractable Unionist opposition. Thus the Unionist perspective: While they may not have brought the Agreement down, they have cauterized it. Their continuing opposition to it rests on the belief that in the act of guaranteeing their position in the United Kingdom, insofar as majority consent would be required to change their status, the Agreement itself, formulated without their knowledge and forced upon them without their consent, alters their status by giving Dublin a voice in the governance of Northern Ireland.

Unionists accept that the Agreement precipitated an identity crisis of sorts in their community, but one that drew them back to their core values – to the belief that they stood alone and would have to work out their future with the knowledge that they could not trust the neighbor on their border or the nation to which they had given their putative allegiance. Their antipathy for the South far outweighs their distaste for the English. In the sense that Hume sees the Unionist versus the-rest-of-Ireland as the "key relationship", the words "key" and "relationship" have antithetical meanings for Unionists. It is up to the two governments, they believe, to admit their failure, to set the Agreement aside, and to call the parties together for talks.

However, Unionist bravado and confidence in the ineffectiveness of the Agreement and self-assurance in the perceptiveness of their analysis is too confident, too self-assured. It belies their sense of powerlessness, of their political future having been taken out of their hands, of their being bereft of easy alternatives and uneasy and uncertain regarding the use of violence. Looking for historical parallels that make a virtue of powerlessness, they take vicarious solace in the march of protest in Eastern Europe, where the silent protest of other majorities, denied their democratic rights for decades, masked their hatred for the manner in which they were oppressed.

Unable to come to terms with what has happened, they have denied it, always able to decipher their realities in terms that validate their assessment of the Agreement. Because they have such a psychological investment in insisting that the Agreement is a failure, Unionists look for vindication of their position and are compelled, therefore, to require that the two governments suspend the operations of the Conference so that discussions for an alternative may begin. But even here, their demands have shifted significantly, from strident ultimatums that the Agreement be abandoned, to less plangent calls for the suspension of the workings of the Conference, to rather hopeful suggestions that a period between meetings of the Conference might be used to temporarily redeploy some of the Secretariat's top level personnel for a couple of months or so. "I sense from Unionists," says John Alderdice, "that if there was [some] kind of act of symbolic generosity, that it might well put them in a position where they felt both motivated to and, indeed, pressed to respond positively in terms of discussion." For politicians like Peter Robinson, the need for talks is beyond urgency and the paralysis of inaction has become the harbinger of defeat. But even when Robinson said that a two-month break between meetings of the Conference would be sufficient to discover if agreement among the North's political parties was possible,[118] there was no enthusiastic rush to agree with him from either side of the divide. Lip service to talks is most pronounced when the prospects of talks are most remote.

● Sinn Fein does maintain a "veto over the entire breadth of manoeuvrability of the SDLP." In the absence of a cease-fire, it poses particular problems for SDLP participation in an internal governance structure. Perceptions of what the security problem is and its relationship to the administration of justice, the widespread unacceptability of the UDR in the Nationalist community – even among moderate Nationalists – and its corresponding widespread acceptability in the Unionist community – even among moderate Unionists – create an unstable basis for devolution. On too many sensitive issues the SDLP in government might find itself in opposition to the sentiments prevailing in its own community. The SDLP would have to consider the political costs of becoming part of an administration that would, perhaps, drive a wedge between it and a sizable segment of the Catholic community, or one that would be required to implement many of the cuts in social services that are the hallmark of Thatcher's privatization programs.

● Sinn Fein/IRA/the armed struggle – whatever one wants to call it – has been the major agent of change during the eighties.

It cannot afford to agree to a cease-fire – it would only marginalize itself and drown in the larger sea of Nationalists. Having survived the appalling massacre at Enniskillen and a hard-to-fathom propensity to shoot mistaken victims, its strength in the hardcore Republican ghettos is virtually immune to challenge. In the longer run, holding its share of the vote in the North is sufficient. Only if that vote were to dramatically soften would the Armalite-ballot box strategy begin to disintegrate. And even if it were to, the primacy of the physical force component would simply reassert itself.

But as long as Sinn Fein can hold an electoral share in the region of thirty percent of the Catholic vote, it retains the critical mass it needs to assert a political leverage that is, in many respects, independent of the armed struggle. The firmer the grip Sinn Fein holds on a substantial part of the Catholic vote, the more difficult it is for the SDLP to join a devolved government; the margin to withstand a potential backlash in the minority community, in the face of some decision of an internal administration, becomes uncomfortably small. Moreover, if up to one-third of the Catholic community continues to reject the jurisdiction of a devolved government, the more specious the claim of the SDLP to have the moral and political authority to speak for the whole community. Indeed, the IRA will never be convinced by the arithmetic of conventional politics. The gun gives it its authenticity: Its rationalization of its mandate for armed struggle denies an understanding of fundamental democratic principles. Its allegiance is not to freedom but to its own conception of history.

● The IRA's campaign is aided by the passive politics of constitutionalists – their unwillingness to compromise. No party accepts responsibility for its inaction because there is no electoral price to be paid for inaction. No party, North or South – except, perhaps, on the extremes – believes that the British government has a policy with regard to Northern Ireland. Moreover, the latter reflect ingrained prejudices rather than considered opinions. Nationalists reject the notion that the implementation of the Anglo-Irish Agreement, in its full sense, amounts to a British policy. Again, they would see it as a declaration of purpose, rather than a set of strategic goals. And this, of course, reinforces Nationalist perceptions that British policy remains one of crisis management with too much emphasis on security – while Unionists perceive it as crisis management with too little emphasis on security. Increasingly, Nationalists, North and South, and Unionists believe that Britain wants out: that this is the real agenda behind the policy vacuum. "My perception," says Dick Spring, "is that the British public opinion has shifted enormously in the sense that the British want to get out of Northern Ireland in a big way. Privately, all of the politicians are saying that." Concomitantly, no opposition party in the South believes that the Irish government has a policy with regard to the North.

Ultimately, however, the success of the Anglo-Irish Agreement will be measured in terms of the extent to which it facilitates a resolution of the often conflicting agendas it poses for the major constitutional players. It may fail to do so. The extent of the segregation of the two communities is almost total; the Agreement, at best, treats the symptoms and not the causes of that segregation; and the best-intentioned structures developed and imposed from without cannot substantially alleviate the wellsprings of a seemingly unyielding and immutable communal division that emanates from deep within. But even if it does fail, it has altered the context for all future policy action. Its enduring importance, therefore, is the fact that it was implemented in the first place.

A Final Reflection

Perhaps "the talk about talks" will generate its own momentum and bring the constitutional parties to the negotiating table. Or perhaps events in Europe will provide the impetus for initiating some sort of dialogue. In 1922, Winston Churchill wrote: "The whole map of Europe has been changed ... The modes of thought of men, the whole outlook on affairs, the grouping of parties, all have encountered violent and tremendous changes in the deluge of the world. But as the deluge subsides and the waters fall short, we see the dreary steeples of Fermanagh and Tyrone emerging once again. The integrity of their quarrel is one of the few institutions that has been unaltered in the cataclysm which has swept the world."[119]

Almost seventy years later, the whole map of Europe has been changed once again. Borders have opened and regimes have collapsed – first in Poland, then in Hungary, then in Bulgaria, and in rapid succession, in East Germany, Czechoslovakia and Romania. Europe was seized with a tumultuous energy, volcano-like in its spontaneous combustions, accelerating the drive towards economic and social integration in the European Community, raising disturbing questions about the seeming inevitability of German reunification – which will come about, all are agreed, only with the freely-given consent of the East German people – and bringing the promise of free elections to countries that had existed under the iron foot of totalitarianism for over forty years.

The impatience of people, now free, to transform their entire societies, to tear down old structures of repression and to replace them with ones that would ensure justice and liberty for all, shattered the old order. The phenomenon of people power became the most important catalyst of change in our time.

But while perestroika brought new freedoms, it brought old problems. Eastern Europe and the U.S.S.R., it is increasingly clear, are, in many respects, not a network of nations but a patchwork of ethnic groups. The new freedoms have become a catalyst for a resurgence of long-suppressed ethnic and nationalist rivalries.

And as these rivalries play themselves out, each group asserting old claims on the past, they will, perhaps, give some perspective to the Northern Ireland conflict, an intractable problem joined by a slew of other intractable problems, but one with a degree of order – its own carefully calibrated rules that keep the violence within acceptable boundaries, for the most part. And perhaps with other ethnic conflicts to refine their reflections, the two communities in Northern Ireland might begin to realize that you cannot create a lasting peace if you empower one minority by creating another. And perhaps they'll learn, too, that they are not so different after all.

REFERENCES

1 Irish Government Publications. "Report of the New Ireland Forum". Dublin: The Stationery Office, 1984.

2 Mr. Charles Haughey quoted in *Irish Times*, 3 May 1984.

3 Mr. Charles Haughey quoted in *Irish Times*, 28 February 1983.

4 See Olivia O'Leary, "Haughey at the Forum," *Magill*, May 1984, pp. 10–14.

5 Dr. Garret FitzGerald quoted in *Irish Times*, 3 May 1984.

6 *Irish Times*, 12 May 1984.

7 *Irish Times*, 12 May 1984.

8 Meeting between Margaret Thatcher and Garret FitzGerald. Joint Communique, 6 November 1981. Reported in *Irish Times*, 7 November 1981.

9 *Irish Times*, 16 November 1985.

10 Irish Government Publications. "Anglo-Irish Agreement". Dublin: The Stationery Office, 1985.

11 Address by Charles Haughey to Dail Eireann, 19 November 1985. Reported in *Irish Times*, 20 November 1985.

12 *Fortnight* and Ulster Television Survey. Reported in *Irish Times*, 25 March 1988.

13 *Irish Times*, 28 July 1982.

14 Austin Currie, former senior SDLP spokesperson (now Fine Gael T.D. in Dail Eireann), quoted in *Fortnight* No. 256 Nov. 1987, p. 7.

15 Address by Seamus Mallon to 1989 SDLP Annual Conference. Reported in *Irish Times*, 4 November 1989.

16 "Sinn Fein/SDLP Talks", January-September 1988. Dublin: Sinn Fein Publicity Department, January 1989, p. 3.

17 *Ibid.*, p. 23.

18 *Ibid.*, p. 11.

19 *Ibid.*, p. 17.

20 Interview with John Hume, 28 August 1986.

21 "Sinn Fein/SDLP Talks", p. 17.

22 *Ibid.*, p. 20.

23 "Sinn Fein/SDLP Talks", p. 19.

24 Interview with John Hume, 22 October 1989.

25 Address by John Hume to 1989 SDLP Annual Conference. Reported in *Irish Times*, 4 November 1989.

26 "Sinn Fein/SDLP Talks", p. 17.

27 John Hume interviewed by Frank Millar in *Irish Times*, 13 January 1989.

28 See interview with John Hume in Padraig O'Malley, *The Uncivil Wars: Ireland Today*. Boston, Mass: Houghton Mifflin Company, 1983, p. 100; Belfast: Blackstaff, 1983, p. 100.

29 "Sinn Fein/SDLP Talks", p. 17.

30 *Ibid.*, pp. 23–24.

31 For example, see O'Malley, *The Uncivil Wars*, pp. 138–141.

32 See O'Malley, *The Uncivil Wars*, pp. 239–240.

33 "Sinn Fein/SDLP Talks", p. 20.

34 Speech and press conference of Tom King in Brussels, 3 December 1985. Reported in *Irish Times*, 4 December 1985.

35 Interview with John Hume, 28 August 1986.

36 Interview with John Hume, 22 October 1989.

37 See O'Malley, *The Uncivil Wars*, pp. 100–102.

38 Interview with John Hume, 28 August 1986.

39 See interview with John Hume in O'Malley, *The Uncivil Wars*, p. 102.

40 See page 57.

41 Interview with Peter Robinson, 29 August 1988.

42 *Ibid.*

43 *Ibid.*

44 Interview with Harold McCusker, 29 July 1986.

45 Interview with Ken Maginnis, 13 July 1986.

116

46 Ian Paisley Address to DUP Annual Conference 1989. Reported in *Irish Times*, 27 November 1988.

47 Interview with Peter Robinson, 29 August 1988.

48 *Ibid*.

49 *Ibid*.

50 *Ibid*.

51 Gerry Adams, *The Politics of Irish Freedom*. Dingle, County Kerry: Brandon, 1986, p. 10.

52 Patrick Bishop and Eamonn Mallie, *The Provisional IRA*. London: Corgi Books, 1988, p. 387.

53 "Sinn Fein/SDLP Talks", p. 4.

54 *Ibid*., p. 13.

55 "Sinn Fein/SDLP Talks", p. 4.

56 *Ibid*., p. 5.

57 *Ibid*.

58 *Ibid*., p. 6.

59 *Ibid*., p. 8.

60 *Ibid*., p. 6.

61 *Ibid*., p. 7.

62 *Ibid*., p. 8.

63 *Ibid*., p. 14.

64 See *An Phoblacht/Republican News*, 6 November 1986.

65 Adams, *op. cit.*, p. 64.

66 Interview with Gerry Adams, 25 March 1985.

67 Interview with Gerry Adams, 30 August 1988.

68 Interview with Gerry Adams, 15 November 1989.

69 Interview with Gerry Adams, 30 August 1988.

70 *Ibid*.

71 Interview with Gerry Adams, 15 November 1989.

72 Interview with Gerry Adams, 30 August 1988.

73 *Ibid*.

74 See page 57.

75 Interview with Gerry Adams, 15 November 1989.

76 See quote from Danny Morrison, *The Uncivil Wars*, p. 278.

77 Interview with Gerry Adams, 15 November 1988.

78 Interview with Gerry Adams, 30 August 1988.

79 Interview with Danny Morrison, 8 November 1989.

80 Interview with Gerry Adams, 15 November 1989.

81 *Ibid.*

82 Interview with John Hume, 28 August 1986.

83 *Irish Times* editorial, 20 January 1988.

84 Reported in *Irish Times*, 29 January 1988.

85 *Irish Times* editorial, 29 January 1988.

86 Interview with Mr. Haughey on "This Week", RTE, 10 January 1988.

87 Garret FitzGerald interviewed by David McKittrick, *The Independent*, 7 June 1989.

88 Speech by the Taoiseach, Mr. Charles J. Haughey, at the annual Wolfe Tone Commemoration at Bodenstown, 11 October 1987. Reported in *Irish Times*, 12 October 1987.

89 Address by the Taoiseach, Mr. Charles J. Haughey, to 1988 Fianna Fail Ard Fheis, 20 February 1988. Reported in *Irish Times*, 22 February 1988.

90 Address by the Taoiseach, Mr. Charles J. Haughey, to the Friends of Fianna Fail, New York, 21 April 1988. Reported in *Irish Times*, 22 April 1988.

91 Address by the Taoiseach, Mr. Charles J. Haughey, to Dail Eireann. See Dail Eireann: *Parliamentary Debates*, 3 November 1989, cols. 1472–1485.

92 *Ibid.*, col. 1478.

93 Address by Party leader Alan Dukes to 1988 Fine Gael Ard Fheis, 5 November 1988. Reported in *Irish Times*, 7 November 1988.

118

94 Address by Leader of the Opposition, Alan Dukes, to Dail Eireann. See Dail Eireann: *Parliamentary Debates*, 23 November 1989, col. 1490.

95 *Ibid.*, col. 1488.

96 Interview with John Hume, 28 August 1986.

97 Address by leader of the Workers' Party, Proinsias de Rossa, to Dail Eireann. See Dail Eireann: *Parliamentary Debates*, 24 November 1989, col. 1734.

98 Quoted in *Irish Times*, 4 November 1989.

99 Quoted in *Irish Times*, 6 November 1989.

100 Address by Peter Brooke to Londonderry/Derry Chamber of Commerce, 28 November 1989. Reported in *Irish Times*, 29 November 1989.

101 Letter from Peter Brooke to author, 14 December 1989.

102 Interview with Peter Brooke, 9 January 1990.

103 Address by the Taoiseach, Mr. Charles J. Haughey, to 1989 Fianna Fail Ard Fheis, 25 February 1989. Reported in *Irish Times*, 27 February 1989.

104 Quoted in *Irish Times*, 4 November 1989.

105 Address by Peter Brooke to Bangor Chamber of Commerce, 9 January 1990. Reported in *Irish Times*, 10 January 1990.

106 *Ibid.*

107 "Towards a New Ireland" issued by the British Labour Party's Front Bench Northern Ireland Team in the House of Commons, Westminster, London, September 1988.

108 *Irish News* editorial, 11 October 1989.

109 Des O'Malley on the BBC's "On the Record", 15 October 1989. Reported in *Irish Times*, 16 October 1989.

110 Interview with Seamus Mallon, 6 January 1990.

111 *Irish Times* editorial, 11 October 1989.

112 James Prior in the House of Commons, Westminster, London, 2 July 1984. Reported in *Irish Times*, 3 July 1984.

113 Statement by Alan Dukes. Reported in *Irish Times*, 1 November 1989.

114 Address by the Taoiseach, Mr. Charles J. Haughey, to Dail Eireann. See Dail Eireann: *Parliamentary Debates*, 23 November 1989, col. 1478.

115 Address by Leader of the Opposition, Alan Dukes, to Dail Eireann. See Dail Eireann: *Parliamentary Debates*, 23 November 1989, col. 1490.

116 An *Irish Times*/MRBI opinion poll found sixty-eight percent of respondents supported the Agreement. Reported in *Irish Times*, 28 November 1989.

117 Interview with John Hume, 28 August 1986.

118 *Irish Times*, 11 December 1989.

119 Winston Churchill quoted in A.T.Q. Stewart, *The Narrow Ground: Aspects of Ulster 1609-1969*. London: Faber & Faber, 1977, p. 14.

NOTES

[1] During a four-week period in November/December 1982, six Irish Catholic Nationalists, all unarmed and some with vague connections to the IRA, were shot dead by members of an anti-terrorist unit of the Royal Ulster Constabulary (RUC). The shootings created a public outcry with accusations that the RUC was engaged in a shoot-to-kill policy. John Stalker, Deputy Chief Constable of the Greater Manchester Police, was appointed to conduct an independent investigation into the circumstances of the seven deaths. Stalker's investigation established that the RUC's accounts of what had happened were pure fabrication; that the officers involved in the shootings were instructed by their superiors to lie, allegedly to protect informant networks; that four of the deaths were possibly revenge killings; that huge sums of money were paid to informants, and that informants were acting, perhaps, as *agents provocateurs* and bounty hunters. Following accusations that he had "consorted with known criminals" in Manchester, Stalker was taken off the case and suspended as Deputy Chief Constable shortly before he could complete the investigation. (He was subsequently cleared of all the charges and reinstated as Deputy Chief Constable.) In January 1988, the Stalker Report on the RUC killings, completed under the direction of Colin Sampson, Chief Constable of the West Yorkshire Police, was submitted to Sir Patrick Mayhew, the British Attorney General, but for national security reasons the findings were not made public and no disciplinary action was taken against RUC officers charged with committing crimes and perverting the course of justice.

[2] Nineteen people died when bombs went off in two Birmingham pubs on 21 November 1974. Six men were given life sentences for the bombing. Subsequently, sufficient evidence of the Birmingham Six's innocence turned up to warrant an appeal being granted. Even when the appeal failed, two events kept the controversy over the Six alive. First, in August 1989 the West Midlands Police's serious crime squad – members of which were involved in the interrogation of the Birmingham Six – was disbanded after allegations that it had fabricated evidence in more recent cases. Second, in October 1989, the Guilford Four – Gerard Conlon, Paul Hill, Carole Richardson, and Patrick Armstrong,

who had been jailed for life for the IRA bombing of pubs in Guilford and Woolwich in 1974 on the strength of confessions – were released after police uncovered evidence that the case against the Four was fabricated, in part, by police officers who investigated the case. The Irish government continues to press for the release of the Six or at the very least for a further investigation into the circumstances of their trial. At the time of going to press, the British Home Secretary, David Waddington, was awaiting the results of a new investigation into "certain aspects of the case" to see whether his further intervention into the convictions of the six men would be justified.

[3] Some of the achievements attributed to the Agreement: the repeal of the Flags and Emblems Act; the decision to demolish substandard housing in Derry and Belfast; the greater powers police have to control parades; reforms in the Emergency Laws that reduce the maximum period police can hold suspects from seventy-two hours to forty-eight; the atrophy of the supergrass system; legislation to prohibit job discrimination; a new code of conduct for the Royal Ulster Constabulary; better procedures for handling complaints against the police; better cross-border security cooperation; and the creation of the International Fund for Ireland.

[4] The OUP and the DUP agreed not to challenge each other's incumbent M.P.s in the special by-elections called in January 1986, after all Unionist M.P.s resigned their seats, and again in the Westminster general elections in June 1987. At the DUP's annual conference in November 1989, the DUP declared that henceforth it would contest seats in all constituencies in which it was clear that a divided Unionist vote would not result in the election of a Nationalist/Republican candidate. The essence of the Unionist pact, Paisley insists, is not its electoral dimension but rather the joint undertaking by the two party leaders not to engage in unilateral talks with the NIO.

[5] Taylor is not alone in believing that the Anglo-Irish Agreement has, in the absence of devolution, facilitated the further integration of Northern Ireland into the rest of the United Kingdom. Among others who hold similar views: Sammy Wilson (DUP); Garret FitzGerald and Alan Dukes (FG); Des O'Malley (PDs); and Eddie McGrady (SDLP).

[6] A bomb packed with about thirty pounds of explosives left inside the community center adjacent to the war memorial blew a gable wall out on top of the crowd that had come to watch the services, killing eleven people – all of them Protestant and all of them civilians – and injuring sixty-three others, many of them seriously. After a thirty-hour silence, the IRA took responsibility for the bombing and expressed regret for it.

[7] For example, in October 1988, access to radio and television by the political wings of paramilitary organizations, including Sinn Fein and the UDA, was restricted. Members of these organizations are prohibited from appearing on TV or being heard on radio. These restrictions applied to both the British Broadcasting Corporation and the Independent Broadcasting Authority. The Elected Authorities (Northern Ireland) Bill, introduced in December 1988, required candidates for district councils or Assembly elections in Northern Ireland to sign a declaration stating that the candidates, if elected, would not express support for proscribed organizations or acts of terrorism. Signing the declaration is a condition of nomination as a candidate. It also changed the present rules of disqualification. It used to be that those sentenced to three or more months imprisonment, without the option of a fine, were disqualified for a period of five years from the date of conviction. Under the new legislations, such persons are disqualified, both while imprisoned and, thereafter, for five years from the date of discharge.

[8] The Prevention of Terrorism bill was introduced to the House of Commons on 28 November 1974, seven days after the Birmingham pub bombings. It was intended as a temporary measure. The Act gives the Home Secretary the right to detain people suspected of terrorist offenses for up to seven days without charges and to expel them from the country by executive decision. The Act had to be renewed every year.

[9] A further example of this kind of powerlessness occurred in August 1989. After allegations emerged that members of the UDR and the RUC were supplying Loyalist paramilitary groups with photomontages and other particulars of suspected members of the IRA, the Irish government called for a full investigation and a fundamental overhauling of the UDR. An investigation was started under the direction of John

Stevens, Deputy Chief Constable of the Cambridgeshire Police, but London rejected Dublin's position on the UDR. The British government also proceeded with plans to issue plastic bullets to the UDR, despite Dublin's vehement opposition. Dublin did wring some concessions: a special unit to screen UDR recruits and to revet serving members; plastic bullets would only be issued if authorized by the commanding officer; and, yet again, RUC accompaniment of UDR patrols was promised. Dublin said "It wished for more progress."

[10] At the time galleys of *Northern Ireland: Questions of Nuance* became available (May 1990), it appeared that Brooke had achieved a break-through and that round-table inter-party talks might begin in the early fall.

[11] On 17 May 1990, David Trimble, the Official Unionist Party's candidate won the by-election in Upper Bann to fill the Westminster parliamentary seat left vacant by the death of Harold McCusker. In the weeks preceding the election, several British ministers and the chair-man of the Conservative Party, Kenneth Baker, canvassed the constitu-ency on behalf of Colette Jones, the Conservative Party candidate. Trimble received 20,507 votes and Jones received 1,038 votes.

BELFAST PUBLIC LIBRARIES

OTHER TITLES

from

THE BLACKSTAFF PRESS

NORTHERN IRELAND

A POLITICAL DIRECTORY 1968–88

W. D. FLACKES
SYDNEY ELLIOTT

First published in 1980, *Northern Ireland: A Political Directory* has established itself as the foremost reference book in its field. This third edition, completely revised and updated, covers in detail the twenty years since the onset of the current troubles.

With an Introduction and Chronology of Events, Alphabetical Dictionary of people, parties, organisations and key places, and sections on Election Results, Systems of Government in Northern Ireland and the Security System, this is an indispensable guide for anyone with a serious interest in Irish politics.

'No better man to compile a political directory of Northern Ireland … impeccably precise in defining political positions of all colours and degrees of stubbornness.'
Sunday Independent

'Immensely useful work by one of the foremost authorities on Northern Ireland and the politics of the region.'
Cork Examiner

198 x 129mm; 448pp; 0 85640 418 7; pb

£9.95

BITING AT THE GRAVE

THE IRISH HUNGER STRIKES AND THE POLITICS OF DESPAIR

PADRAIG O'MALLEY

'A book equal to the pity and terror of its subject. Padraig O'Malley simplifies nothing, extenuates nothing, and scrutinizes everything. This is not only a heartfelt narrative but a sustained exercise of moral and political intelligence.'

Seamus Heaney

'Fasting to death has been a grim Irish ritual from pre-Christian times to Mrs Thatcher's. In this important book, by placing the Maze Prison hunger strikes of 1980 and 1981 in the context of myth, politics, and history, Padraig O'Malley makes comprehensible the perplexing sacrifice of ten lives.'

Brenda Maddox, author of *Nora*

'This is not a book on the hunger strike; it's a book about the Irish that just happens to be anchored in that awful time, a time that O'Malley dissects with wonderful and horrible precision. I turned each page with wonder, even reading stories I already knew. O'Malley's prose is graceful, a pleasure to read ... a terrific piece of work.'

John Conroy, author of *Belfast Diary*

198 x 129 mm; 320 pp; 0-85640-453-5; pb
£9.95

ORDERING BLACKSTAFF BOOKS

All Blackstaff Press books are available through bookshops. In the case of difficulty, however, orders can be made directly to the publisher. Indicate clearly the title and number of copies required and send order with your name and address to:

CASH SALES

Blackstaff Press Limited
3 Galway Park
Dundonald
Belfast BT16 0AN
Northern Ireland

Please enclose a remittance to the value of the cover price plus: £1.00 for the first book plus 60p per copy for each additional book ordered to cover postage and packing. Payment should be made in sterling by UK personal cheque, postal order, sterling draft or inter-national money order, made payable to Blackstaff Press Limited.

Applicable only in the UK and Republic of Ireland
Full catalogue available on request